Transformative Entrepreneurship in the Global Landscape

Diala Kabbara

Transformative Entrepreneurship in the Global Landscape

A Gender Perspective

Diala Kabbara
Department of Economics and Management
University of Pavia
Pavia, Italy

ISBN 978-3-031-77140-8   ISBN 978-3-031-77141-5 (eBook)
https://doi.org/10.1007/978-3-031-77141-5

© The Editor(s) (if applicable) and The Author(s), under exclusive license to Springer Nature Switzerland AG 2025

This work is subject to copyright. All rights are solely and exclusively licensed by the Publisher, whether the whole or part of the material is concerned, specifically the rights of translation, reprinting, reuse of illustrations, recitation, broadcasting, reproduction on microfilms or in any other physical way, and transmission or information storage and retrieval, electronic adaptation, computer software, or by similar or dissimilar methodology now known or hereafter developed.
The use of general descriptive names, registered names, trademarks, service marks, etc. in this publication does not imply, even in the absence of a specific statement, that such names are exempt from the relevant protective laws and regulations and therefore free for general use.
The publisher, the authors and the editors are safe to assume that the advice and information in this book are believed to be true and accurate at the date of publication. Neither the publisher nor the authors or the editors give a warranty, expressed or implied, with respect to the material contained herein or for any errors or omissions that may have been made. The publisher remains neutral with regard to jurisdictional claims in published maps and institutional affiliations.

This Palgrave Macmillan imprint is published by the registered company Springer Nature Switzerland AG.
The registered company address is: Gewerbestrasse 11, 6330 Cham, Switzerland

If disposing of this product, please recycle the paper.

To my Mother Siham and my Father Abed-Razzak
To my Husband Houssam, my Daughter Yara, my Sons Omar and Karim
Thank you for your continuous support and encouragement!

Praise for *Transformative Entrepreneurship in the Global Landscape*

"We are living in an era marked by unprecedented challenges and opportunities. In this context, the role of entrepreneurship has never been more critical and has assumed new meanings and nuances. The intertwining of innovation, digital transformation, and sustainability issues redefines the landscape of business and society, pushing us towards a more inclusive and equitable future. This book—*Transformative Entrepreneurship in the Global Landscape: A Gender Perspective*—contributes to the debate by investigating intersections and synergies between these forces, focusing on the pivotal role of inclusion in modern and global ecosystems.

From the initial conceptualisation by economist Richard Cantillon in 1730 to the seminal contribution by Joseph Schumpeter in 1934, a long time has passed, but the term "entrepreneurship" seems to have weathered the centuries, remaining more or less intact across eras, preserving its core meaning. Yet, as mentioned earlier, the world has truly changed.

The term was originally associated with economic growth through innovation and job creation. However, the author of this book Diala Kabbara has the insightful intuition to highlight that—today—starting new ventures by seizing latent opportunities and addressing risky challenges that no one else would take on is much more than just creating jobs and products. Now, entrepreneurship is the art of generating new value that is simultaneously economic, social, and environmental, aiming towards a better world and overcoming the dichotomy between for-profit and non-profit. This expanded view of entrepreneurship is particularly relevant in an era characterised by global interconnectedness, social and health crises, and the rapid advancement of exponential technologies. At the heart of this transition lies the concept of *transformative entrepreneurship*, as a construct well debated and explored in this book.

In doing so, the author assigns a key relevance to inclusive forms of entrepreneurship. In particular, inclusion in entrepreneurship is interpreted not merely as a matter of fairness; it is a strategic imperative. Diverse perspectives and experiences are crucial drivers of innovation. When individuals from different backgrounds come together, they bring unique insights and approaches to problem-solving, leading to more creative and effective solutions. This is particularly important in the context of transformative entrepreneurship, where the goal is to tackle complex and multifaceted challenges. Gender inequality, for instance, remains a pervasive issue in many parts of the world. Despite these obstacles, women entrepreneurs are making significant contributions to transforming the global economy from new angles, particularly in sectors such as international entrepreneurship, digitalisation and sustainability.

Similarly, migrant entrepreneurship emerges in this book as a powerful and effective force for fostering innovation grounded in the interplay between economic, social, and even environmental new values. Talents who move from one country, region, or area to another—typically for reasons such as seeking better economic opportunities, escaping conflict or persecution, reuniting with family, or even pursuing a better education—bring with them unique skills, perspectives, and networks that contribute to a heterogeneous mix of competencies and values, leading to new perspectives and disruptive solutions. In the context of the new globalisation, where cross-border movements of people, goods, and ideas are more fluid than ever, migrant entrepreneurs can play a vital role in fostering cross-cultural exchange and driving economic dynamism. However, like women entrepreneurs, migrants often face significant barriers, including legal restrictions, discrimination, and limited access to resources. Addressing these challenges is essential for unleashing the full potential of migrant entrepreneurship and ensuring that it contributes to the transition towards new views on sustainable development.

This book aims to provide a comprehensive exploration of these themes, offering insights into how transformative entrepreneurship can drive positive change in the world. It brings together perspectives from a diverse group of scholars, practitioners, and entrepreneurs, highlighting the critical role of inclusion in the entrepreneurial process. Through a combination of theoretical analysis and case studies, the book seeks to shed light on the ways in which innovation, digital transformation, and sustainability can be harnessed to create a more inclusive and equitable world.

One of the key themes explored in this book to achieve the above-mentioned goal is the role of digital transformation and exponential technologies in driving and scaling transformative entrepreneurship. Digital technologies have become a powerful enabler of innovation and diversity, breaking down barriers to entry and creating new opportunities for entrepreneurs around the world. The rise of exponential technologies—such as artificial intelligence, blockchain, and the Internet of Things—presents both opportunities and challenges for transformative entrepreneurship. This revolution has democratised access to information, resources, and markets, allowing entrepreneurs from diverse backgrounds to participate in the global economy. The above-mentioned technologies have the potential to revolutionise industries, create new markets, and address global challenges in ways that were previously unimaginable. However, they also raise important questions about ethics, equity, and inclusivity.

Whether you are a scholar, an entrepreneur, a policymaker, or simply someone interested in the future of business and society, this book will inspire you to think critically about the role of entrepreneurship in shaping the world we want to live in. Diala Kabbara has redesigned this complex puzzle composed of numerous variables and implications, capturing the central messages and fundamental lessons that should inspire every modern entrepreneur, from any part of the world, in the dream of deeply transforming the society around us towards models of prosperity based on new values. We need it, and this book is a concrete contribution in that direction."

—Prof. Stefano Denicolai, *Head of Institute for Transformative Innovation Research (ITIR)—University of Pavia*

Contents

1 Introduction   1

2 Transformative Entrepreneurship and Global Transformation   9

3 Global Female Entrepreneurship: Exploring The Motivations and Challenges   35

4 Digital Entrepreneurship: Empowering Female Entrepreneurs   63

5 Sustainable Entrepreneurship: The Engagement of Female Entrepreneurs   85

6 Social Transformative Entrepreneurship: The Emergence of Female Migrant Entrepreneurs   113

Conclusion   135

Index   143

About the Author

Diala Kabbara is an assistant professor at the University of Pavia, Italy. She holds a PhD in Business Administration Management from the University of Pavia. She has over twelve years of research and teaching experience. Her research works revolve around international entrepreneurship, female entrepreneurship, and international management. Her papers were presented at international conferences and published in internationally ranked scientific journals such as *International Business Review, Journal of International Management, International entrepreneurship and Management Journal,* and *Journal of Business Research*. She served on the editorial boards of books published by Springer and World Scientific.

LIST OF FIGURES

Fig. 1.1	Dimensions of transformative entrepreneurship in the global landscape. (Source: The author)	4
Fig. 2.1	World ecological deficit and reserves. (Source: Global Footprint Network (2023). Data footprint network https://data.footprintnetwork.org/#/)	17
Fig. 2.2	Internet users around the world. (Sources: IMF, World Economic Outlook (Washington, DC: International Monetary Fund, 2023); International Telecommunications Union (2022), Global Connectivity Report 2022, https://www.itu.int/itu-d/reports/statistics/global-connectivityreport-2022/; Internet World Stats, Internet Usage Statistics, 2023, www.internetworldstats.com)	19
Fig. 2.3	The evolution of global migration in the last years. (Source: UN DESA, 2021)	27
Fig. 3.1	Start-up motivations by gender. (*Source*: Global Entrepreneurship Monitor (GEM) 2022/2023 Women's Entrepreneurship Report: Challenging Bias and Stereotypes. https://www.gemconsortium.org/file/open?fileId=51352)	42
Fig. 5.1	Sustainability awareness, priorities, and practices for entrepreneurs by gender. (*Source*: Global Entrepreneurship Monitor (GEM) 2022/2023 Women's Entrepreneurship Report: Challenging Bias and Stereotypes. https://www.gemconsortium.org/file/open?fileId=51352)	97

List of Tables

Table 2.1	Some definitions of digital transformation	22
Table 6.1	Different entrepreneurship streams related to migration	117

CHAPTER 1

Introduction

Abstract The global business landscape has experienced unprecedented disruptions and challenges, particularly for female entrepreneurship and international business. This topic of global transformation and its impact on female entrepreneurship and international business is quickly gaining momentum. Internationalisation and globalisation are essential tactics for any company hoping to expand abroad. Female international entrepreneurship has become an interesting field of research and practice, as females are changing cultures and creating wealth for their countries. Existing female international entrepreneurship research has underlined that women have struggled to break the "glass ceiling" and run their businesses. This chapter introduces the relevance of the topic and the aim of this book, which is to understand how female international entrepreneurs interpret and respond to global transformation and how the transformation represents a creative endeavour in which opportunities arise and are exploited.

Keywords International opportunities • Sustainable development • Transformative entrepreneurship • Glass ceiling • Global transformation

In recent years, the global business landscape has witnessed uncommon disruptions and challenges that have transformed the entrepreneurship

© The Author(s), under exclusive license to Springer Nature Switzerland AG 2025
D. Kabbara, *Transformative Entrepreneurship in the Global Landscape*, https://doi.org/10.1007/978-3-031-77141-5_1

and international business game (Yu et al., 2021), particularly the female business (Alhajri & Aloud, 2024; Ughetto et al., 2020). For instance, the COVID-19 pandemic, energy crises, climate change (Initiative, 2021), gender inequality, geopolitical tensions and conflicts are some examples of these disruptions. Undoubtedly, these global disruptions can change the cross-border activities of the companies (Denicolai et al., 2021), providing both entrepreneurial and internationalisation opportunities and challenges, mainly for female entrepreneurs. Due to these global disruptions (on various levels), the business world has experienced a global transformation, including technological advancements (Gong & Ribiere, 2021; Zahra et al., 2023), greater awareness of environmental sustainability (Theodoraki et al., 2022; Xie et al., 2024), the emergence of start-ups working in the informal economy, the advancement of gender equality and inclusivity, and a rise in migration flow (Sinkovics & Reuber, 2021; Villares-Varela et al., 2017).

1.1 Relevance of the Topic

The topic of global transformation and its impact on female entrepreneurship and international business is quickly gaining momentum. It will soon be one of the hottest issues in the fields of innovation studies, environmental and sustainability studies, and female business and management studies. In recent years, a body of literature has grown, mainly from the point of view of policy and practitioners. The academic contributions to this topic are still few, especially if compared to the high relevance of the topic. In particular, a comprehensive analysis of what a transformation entails, especially for female entrepreneurs, and how it can be tackled is still missing.

In response to such transformation, entrepreneurial and international firms must make strategic transformation decisions and switch to more digital, flexible, sustainable and agile business models to keep up with the latest trends and provide a broader outreach to new customers and opportunities in international markets. As such, it calls for integrating new technologies into the firm's operation, incorporating sustainable practices in their business model that align with the sustainable development goals (SDGs). As other strategic decisions, it also calls for launching new international entrepreneurial firms—founded by females—well aligned with the recent changes to economic geography (Pergelova et al., 2019) and the popularisation of inclusive business practices—to achieve economic and financial autonomy, self-achievement and emancipation (Rindova et al., 2009) for marginalised people. Entrepreneurship and international business have enormous transformative power for nations to generate economic growth, embrace pluralism and encompass minorities; however, this transformative force must consider and adjust to several forms and aspects of a global transformation. Among these transformations and impacts on business, the book explores entrepreneurship transformation as a response to the recent global disruptions from a female entrepreneur's perspective

1.2 Aim of the Book

The book aims to examine entrepreneurship's transformative impact on women through their entrepreneurial processes (Johannisson, 2011; Steyaert, 2007) and how these transformations empower female entrepreneurship, addressing some main gaps in the literature. The book aims to elucidate the transformative and emancipatory nature (Atarah et al., 2023; McAdam et al., 2020; Rindova et al., 2009) of the entrepreneurial experience for female entrepreneurs in light of the recent global transformation. The book also aims to understand better how female (international) entrepreneurs interpret and respond to global transformation and how the transformation (digital, social, sustainable) represents a creative endeavour in which opportunities arise and are exploited (please see Fig. 1.1). The book addresses the different forms and aspects of transformation to understand interventions and strategies of female entrepreneurs (Berger & Kuckertz, 2016) to advance sustainable and inclusive economic development. This book addresses this topic, and more precisely, it overviews different practices of transformation in a number of female cases in various countries and industries and provides evidence of their strategies to cope with global transformations, their strengths and weaknesses, the opportunities they address, and the threats they have to face. The data about the female case studies was retrieved from secondary published data.

The global transformation has affected every business across all industries and is independent of the manager's or entrepreneur's gender. This book emphasises how global disruptions and transformations have created challenges and opportunities for transformative entrepreneurs (Harris, 2012), not only for male entrepreneurs but also for female entrepreneurs around the globe. Global transformation and transformative entrepreneurship around the globe have also affected female entrepreneurial activities and empowered female entrepreneurship, a topic—to the best of the author's knowledge—that is still overlooked in the transformative

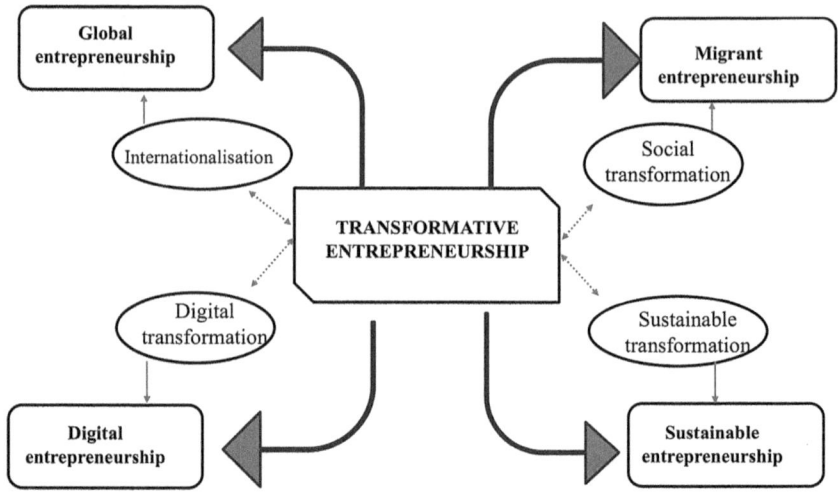

Fig. 1.1 Dimensions of transformative entrepreneurship in the global landscape. (Source: The author)

literature. The book addresses some Sustainable Development Goals (SDGs). More specifically, it addresses issues related to SDG 5 (gender equality) and SDG 10 (reduced inequalities) as it discusses gender perspectives in transformative entrepreneurship.

Entrepreneurship can best deploy its potential for inclusivity and transformativity (Brush et al., 2022; de Bruin & Swail, 2024) in the case of female migrant entrepreneurs (Kabbara et al., 2025; Aman et al., 2024; Sachdeva & Ozga, 2024; Villares-Varela & Essers, 2019), female sustainable entrepreneurs (Rahayu, 2024), and female digital entrepreneurs (Alhajri & Aloud, 2024; Ughetto et al., 2020). More research on female entrepreneurship promises to enrich the content and extend the boundaries of the discipline, particularly by adopting a processual approach that situates the dynamics of entrepreneurial phenomena within their unique contexts (Matricano, 2023).

1.3 Structure of the Book

The book is divided into six chapters, as it is addressed below.

The introduction and the aim of the book are addressed in Chap. 1.

Large-scale disruptions have given rise to problems like pandemics, migration, and climate change. Social, digital, and sustainable transformations are just a few of the significant multifaceted changes in business processes that are included in this transformation. What is the essence of transformative entrepreneurship? What are the primary global challenges and disruptions? Which are the various global transformation typologies? These research questions will be covered in Chap. 2.

Internationalisation and globalisation are essential tactics for any company hoping to expand abroad. (Female) global entrepreneurship has become an interesting field of research and practice, as females are changing cultures and creating wealth for their countries. Existing female international entrepreneurship research has underlined that Women have struggled to break the "glass ceiling" and run their own. In an era of global transformation and advanced technologies, what are the drivers for female global entrepreneurship? How do female international entrepreneurs develop international entrepreneurial opportunities to create multiple value creation? These research questions will be addressed in Chap. 3.

Digital technologies are considered an essential source of transformation in the international business and entrepreneurial environment and provide more opportunities for SMEs and entrepreneurs. The book addresses the advancements and transformations brought about by digital technologies, including the rise of social media platforms, digital platforms, and Artificial Intelligence. How can (female) entrepreneurs leverage digital technologies to keep up with the latest worldwide trends? How does the adoption of digital transformation within an organisation affect it globally? These research questions will be covered in Chap. 4.

Climate change and the impact of tensions on global sourcing are posing significant challenges to all types of companies in a wide variety of sectors and nations. Why are companies and (female) entrepreneurs willing to embrace the circular economy and adapt to the environmental transformation? How do female entrepreneurs implement sustainable practices in their business activities to adhere to sustainable development goals? These research questions will be addressed in Chap. 5.

A significant and growing stream in international entrepreneurship is linked to migration flows due to the increased number of migrants and refugees globally, making the case for addressing the impact of migration on international business highly relevant. This trend is expected to increase, particularly in light of the recent wars (in Europe and in the Middle East). How do (female) migrant entrepreneurs manage the trade-off between opportunities and constraints in the host countries? How do they cope with their liabilities to undertake international entrepreneurial activities? These research questions will be addressed in Chap. 6.

References

Alhajri, A., & Aloud, M. (2024). Female digital entrepreneurship: A structured literature review. *International Journal of Entrepreneurial Behavior & Research*, *30*(2/3), 369–397.

Aman, R., Elo, M., Ahokangas, P., & Zhang, X. (2024). Empowering migrant women's entrepreneurship: Stakeholder perspectives from the entrepreneurial ecosystem. *International Journal of Entrepreneurial Behavior & Research*.

Atarah, B. A., Finotto, V., Nolan, E., & van Stel, A. (2023). Entrepreneurship as emancipation: A process framework for female entrepreneurs in resource-constrained environments. *Journal of Small Business and Enterprise Development*, *30*(4), 734–758.

Berger, E. S., & Kuckertz, A. (2016). Female entrepreneurship in startup ecosystems worldwide. *Journal of Business Research*, *69*(11), 5163–5168.

Brush, C., Eddleston, K., Edelman, L., Manolova, T., McAdam, M., & Rossi-Lamastra, C. (2022). Catalyzing change: Innovation in women's entrepreneurship. *Strategic Entrepreneurship Journal*, *16*(2), 243–254.

de Bruin, A., & Swail, J. (2024). Advancing gender inclusivity: Moving entrepreneurial ecosystems onto new paths. *International Journal of Gender and Entrepreneurship*.

Denicolai, S., Zucchella, A., & Magnani, G. (2021). Internationalization, digitalization, and sustainability: Are SMEs ready? A survey on synergies and substituting effects among growth paths. *Technological Forecasting and Social Change*, *166*, 120650.

Gong, C., & Ribiere, V. (2021). Developing a unified definition of digital transformation. *Technovation*, *102*, 102217.

Harris, J. A. (2012). *Transformative entrepreneurs: How Walt Disney, Steve Jobs, Muhammad Yunus, and other innovators succeeded*. Springer.

Initiative, C. G. R. (2021). *Circularity gap report 2021*: Circularity Gap Reporting Initiative.

Johannisson, B. (2011). Towards a practice theory of entrepreneuring. *Small Business Economics*, *36*, 135–150.

Kabbara, D., Suárez-Ortega, S. M., & Zucchella, A. (2025). "Developing entrepreneurial opportunities through multi-layered liabilities: the experiences of female migrant entrepreneurs". *The International Entrepreneurship and Management Journal*, *21*(1), 1–32. https://doi.org/10.1007/s11365-024-01010-3.

Matricano, D. (2023). Entrepreneurship: Shaping the future! The Manifesto. *International Entrepreneurship and Management Journal*, 1–11.

McAdam, M., Crowley, C., & Harrison, R. T. (2020). Digital girl: Cyberfeminism and the emancipatory potential of digital entrepreneurship in emerging economies. *Small Business Economics*, *55*, 349–362.

Pergelova, A., Manolova, T., Simeonova-Ganeva, R., & Yordanova, D. (2019). Democratizing entrepreneurship? Digital technologies and the internationalization of female-led SMEs. *Journal of Small Business Management, 57*(1), 14–39.

Rahayu, N. S. (2024). Assessing the determinant factors affecting green entrepreneurial intention among female entrepreneurs in Indonesia. *Cogent Business & Management, 11*(1), 2378919.

Rindova, V., Barry, D., & Ketchen, D. J., Jr. (2009). Entrepreneuring as emancipation. *Academy of Management Review, 34*(3), 477–491.

Sachdeva, D., & Ozga, J. (2024). Female immigrant entrepreneurs from developing and developed countries: Multi-level approach paving a path to being a successful entrepreneur in Germany. In *Migration and entrepreneurship in the global context: Case studies, processes and practices* (pp. 307–339). Springer.

Sinkovics, N., & Reuber, A. R. (2021). Beyond disciplinary silos: A systematic analysis of the migrant entrepreneurship literature. *Journal of World Business, 56*(4), 101223.

Steyaert, C. (2007). 'Entrepreneuring' as a conceptual attractor? A review of process theories in 20 years of entrepreneurship studies. *Entrepreneurship and Regional Development, 19*(6), 453–477.

Theodoraki, C., Dana, L.-P., & Caputo, A. (2022). Building sustainable entrepreneurial ecosystems: A holistic approach. *Journal of Business Research, 140*, 346–360.

Ughetto, E., Rossi, M., Audretsch, D., & Lehmann, E. E. (2020). Female entrepreneurship in the digital era. *Small Business Economics, 55*(2), 305–312.

Villares-Varela, M., & Essers, C. (2019). Women in the migrant economy. A positional approach to contextualize gendered transnational trajectories. *Entrepreneurship & Regional Development, 31*(3–4), 213–225.

Villares-Varela, M., Ram, M., & Jones, T. (2017). Female immigrant global entrepreneurship: From invisibility to empowerment? *The Routledge Companion to Global Female Entrepreneurship*, 342–357.

Xie, J., Abbass, K., & Li, D. (2024). Advancing eco-excellence: Integrating stakeholders' pressures, environmental awareness, and ethics for green innovation and performance. *Journal of Environmental Management, 352*, 120027.

Yu, Z., Razzaq, A., Rehman, A., Shah, A., Jameel, K., & Mor, R. S. (2021). Disruption in global supply chain and socio-economic shocks: A lesson from COVID-19 for sustainable production and consumption. *Operations Management Research*, 1–16.

Zahra, S. A., Liu, W., & Si, S. (2023). How digital technology promotes entrepreneurship in ecosystems. *Technovation, 119*, 102457.

CHAPTER 2

Transformative Entrepreneurship and Global Transformation

Abstract In the last decade, the business world has undergone a global transformation due to global disruptions on various levels. For instance, significant disturbances and other macro-environmental events define our future world and strongly affect society, the economy, business, and the natural environment. Among these disturbances, we can cite revolutionary technological advances, deteriorating natural environment, climate change, sustainability, shifting demographics, and international migration. From managerial and operational considerations, these disruptions will affect specific value chain activities such as market research, R&D, sourcing, production, marketing, distribution, etc. In pursuing new opportunities that emerged from these global trends, firms can develop new products and services (via R&D, new product development), create new markets (via internationalisation), or penetrate more deeply into existing markets. This transformation (digital, social, sustainable) represents a creative endeavour in which international business opportunities arise and are exploited. Firms, (female) entrepreneurs and institutions are coevolving toward adapting to global transformation. Additionally, policymakers in various regions are becoming more aware of the global transformation trend. This chapter will introduce the concept of transformative entrepreneurship and other related typologies. It will also address some of the main global disruptions (such as the COVID-19 pandemic, artificial intelligence and climate change), as well as the global transformation typologies.

© The Author(s), under exclusive license to Springer Nature Switzerland AG 2025
D. Kabbara, *Transformative Entrepreneurship in the Global Landscape*, https://doi.org/10.1007/978-3-031-77141-5_2

Keywords Transformative entrepreneurship • Global disruptions • Digital transformation • Sustainable transformation • Social transformation • Inclusivity

2.1 Definitions

2.1.1 Definition of Transformative Entrepreneurship

As mentioned in the previous sections, in recent years, the global business landscape has undergone a complex system and has witnessed uncommon disruptions and challenges transforming the entrepreneurship game (Castro et al., 2024; Harris, 2012; Ratten & Jones, 2018), particularly the female business (Kogut & Mejri, 2021). A complex system is defined by Madelin and Ringrose (2016, p. 18) where "no one can have a complete map of the actors and forces at play, the system's behaviour is not simply the sum of the behaviour of those parts, feedback loops surprise us and change the behaviour of the system, the system is 'autopoietic': behaving in a self-driven way and not just in ways we have yet to understand." In response to such transformation and complex systems, entrepreneurial firms are making strategic transformation decisions and switching to more flexible and sustainable business models to keep up with the latest trends and provide a broader outreach to new customers and opportunities in international markets. Transformative entrepreneurship is defined as 'entrepreneurial activities that create positive financial and social well-being ripple effects – intended or unintended – for individuals, collectives, communities and society' (Giraldo et al., 2020, p. 1). Moreover, (Miller & Collier, 2010, p. 85) defines transformational entrepreneurship "as the creation of an innovative virtue-based organisation for the purpose of shifting resources out of an area of lower and into an area of higher purpose and greater value under conditions requiring a holistic perspective. Transformational entrepreneurship transcends economic terms and emphasises the centrality and value of people, their vocations, and the many levels of relationality involved in entrepreneurship, in addition to the technical aspects of the business". The goal of the transformative entrepreneurship field is to develop a comprehensive and heuristic approach that can serve as a solid foundation for future socio-economic growth by investigating and discovering better ways to address present and future challenges.

Transformative entrepreneurship entails the establishment and expansion of new businesses aimed at affecting substantial societal and global economic changes. This approach prioritises making the world a better place over mere profit maximisation, reflecting a shift towards value-driven business practices. Entrepreneurs who aspire to generate significant impact and instigate change in society, the environment, or both are at the forefront of this transformative movement (Formica, 2023). They embody the principles of visionary leadership and commitment to sustainable development, leveraging their entrepreneurial ventures as platforms for addressing some of the world's most pressing issues. Corporate entrepreneurship, or intrapreneurship, plays a pivotal role in this context by fostering innovation and strategic renewal within established companies. This internal entrepreneurial spirit encourages organisations to explore new markets, develop innovative products, and pursue transformative business models, thereby contributing to societal and economic progress on a broader scale. The importance of transformative entrepreneurship is widely recognised by scholars and practitioners, particularly within the context of international entrepreneurship. Large-scale global challenges such as poverty, inequality, climate change, and the disruptive potential of emerging technologies can be effectively mitigated through transformative entrepreneurial initiatives. This form of entrepreneurship not only has the potential to generate profit but also plays a crucial role in creating employment opportunities, improving quality of life, and fostering societal advancement through innovative solutions that transcend national boundaries. The concept emphasises a global perspective, encouraging entrepreneurs to consider the broader implications of their ventures and to seek ways to contribute to international development and cooperation.

Linking transformative entrepreneurship with international entrepreneurship underscores the global perspective. International entrepreneurs play a significant role in addressing complex challenges on a global scale, and their ventures often transcend borders. Transformative international entrepreneurship focuses on businesses that are committed to driving positive change not only within their home countries but also on an international level. This synergy between entrepreneurship and internationalisation is crucial for amplifying the impact of transformative initiatives, enabling them to reach and benefit a wider audience across different cultural and geographical contexts. Corporate entrepreneurship further amplifies this impact by leveraging the resources, reach, and capabilities of established organisations to pursue innovative ventures that align with transformative goals on an international scale.

The field of entrepreneurship and innovation has recently devoted substantial attention to the dynamic and multifaceted concept of transformative international entrepreneurship. This emerging discourse seeks to redefine the essence of entrepreneurial activity, proposing a more holistic and impact-oriented approach. By emphasising the pivotal role of international entrepreneurship in driving positive social, economic, and environmental change, transformative entrepreneurship marks a distinct departure from traditional entrepreneurial practices. This paradigm shift towards transformative entrepreneurship underscores a broader societal recognition of the pressing need for innovative and sustainable solutions to global challenges. It represents a departure from conventional business models focused primarily on financial gain, advocating for a balanced integration of profit and purpose. Digital innovation entrepreneurship, a domain closely linked to international entrepreneurship, is increasingly intertwined with technology and innovation on a global scale. Digital innovation entrepreneurship focuses on businesses that leverage technological breakthroughs to disrupt established markets, develop fresh business strategies, and enhance overall efficiency, benefiting both local and international arenas. Scholars like Teece (2018) have explored the transformative potential of digital innovation entrepreneurship in reshaping industries and fostering international economic growth. This convergence of digital technology and entrepreneurship is pivotal for catalysing significant shifts in how societies operate, communicate, and grow economically, reflecting a broader trend towards a more interconnected and digitally enabled world. Within the realm of corporate entrepreneurship, digital innovation plays a crucial role in driving internal transformation and adaptation, allowing traditional companies to remain competitive and relevant in an ever-changing global marketplace.

There is an ongoing discourse on transformative entrepreneurship's role in shaping a future that is more innovative and interconnected on a global scale. Through this detailed exploration, it is important to illuminate the pathways through which transformative (female) entrepreneurs can harness digital technologies, sustainable practices, and inclusive strategies to create lasting impacts across the globe.

2.1.2 Definition of Inclusive Entrepreneurship

Inclusive entrepreneurship can be defined as the engagement of underrepresented groups in business with the goal of assisting them in resolving their social and economic issues.

Inclusive entrepreneurship aims to unleash the creative potential and help underrepresented groups, primarily youth, women, seniors, immigrants, and people with disabilities. To achieve economic self-sufficiency that benefits both the group and the community as a whole. This concept and practice were developed. After the establishment of a start-up project for individuals with disabilities in 2008, the OECD and the European Union started a few initiatives centred on inclusive entrepreneurship of marginalised populations. The most well-known project is called COPIE (Community for Practice on Inclusive Entrepreneurship), which aims to promote inclusive entrepreneurship by creating useful toolkits. Three reports on policies for inclusive entrepreneurship have already been released by the OECD and the European Commission in collaboration (OECD/The European Commission, 2013, 2014, 2015). In the last few years, governments and politicians in Europe and around the world have shown a strong interest in inclusive entrepreneurship, with support from organisations such as the European Commission and others.

Inclusive entrepreneurship aims to guarantee equal opportunities for individuals to establish and manage businesses, regardless of their personal traits and backgrounds. Inclusive entrepreneurship policies aim to promote the establishment and development of businesses by groups that are typically underrepresented in entrepreneurship. These groups that are under-represented in entrepreneurship include migrants, ethnic minorities, people who identify as having disabilities, women, and those with low educational attainment (Blackburn & Smallbone, 2014) such as women, young people, migrants, seniors, and the unemployed. These groups often face higher-than-average obstacles when it comes to starting their own businesses.

The current changes and relevance of entrepreneurship at the national and international level for economic growth, social impact, and environmental degradation highlight the need for more analysis of entrepreneurial typologies and value creations.

Building upon migrant, international, and female entrepreneurship literature, this book aims to cast a light on the main types of transformative entrepreneurship and drivers cited in the literature and how (female) entrepreneurs create multiple value creation at the social, economic, and environmental levels (Kabbara, 2023). In particular, the book reveals the existence of four types of female entrepreneurship: "female migrant entrepreneur," "female digital entrepreneur," "female sustainable entrepreneur," and which have emerged from the phenomena of "migration," "digitalisation," and "sustainability".

2.1.3 Definition of Informal Entrepreneurship

Around 2 billion people, or 60% of all workers globally, work in the informal economy, which accounts for 80% of all businesses (UNDP, 2022). In the non-agricultural labour force, at least 30% of women work for themselves in the informal sector globally; according to the World Bank (2019), at least 30 per cent of women in the non-agricultural labour force are self-employed in the informal sector worldwide. This percentage is 63% in Africa (WorldBank, 2019).

The concept of informal entrepreneurship has drawn attention in social sciences (Salvi et al., 2023; Webb et al., 2020; Welter et al., 2015). These business owners undertake entrepreneurial activities in a socially acceptable way while avoiding certain legal obligations related to the supply of products and services in a particular Nation (such as off-book commercial transactions and unregistered operations (Salvi et al., 2023).

Despite irregularities in conducting business, informal activities play a crucial role in many economies, particularly in developing countries, varying widely across different regions and sectors. Informal activities are a means of survival for many, providing livelihood on the one hand and opening economic opportunities for individuals on the other. In both ways, they contribute to local economic development.

Recent studies explain the informal sector as a heterogeneous structure in which informality can be an opportunity for some at a specific time, while for others, it is a necessity and a survival strategy (Canelas, 2019; Fairlie & Fossen, 2018; Günther & Launov, 2012; Harati, 2013). As a necessity, some individuals turn to informal entrepreneurship when they lack formal employment options or face economic hardship, thus operating a survival strategy. As an opportunity, informal entrepreneurs often identify market niches or unmet needs that may not be addressed by formal businesses. They seize these opportunities to fill gaps in the market. It becomes a way to experiment with new ventures and exploit a business idea with lower costs and quicker times for activities that require fewer resources and capital compared to formal businesses. This makes it more accessible to individuals with limited financial means.

A relevant part of informal entrepreneurship is represented by the role of women in promoting new business ventures (Bonnet et al., 2019). For many women, informal entrepreneurship can be a means of economic empowerment, providing them with financial independence and leading to self-sufficiency (Hearle et al., 2019). Undertaking entrepreneurial activities in the informal economy can also provide several relevant outcomes for the female entrepreneur at the individual level, like autonomy and independence as well as a family work life balance (Xheneti et al., 2019).

There are some distinctive contextual aspects of being a female informal entrepreneur. The limited access to resources such as finance, technology, and training pushes women—more than men—towards informal entrepreneurship. Aspects such as social and cultural norms, networking, and support systems can be obstacles for women when starting a new business or making it grow.

Women may view their informal business ventures as more socially acceptable, particularly if they indicate close proximity to their homes and the needs of their families. If female entrepreneurship stays in "the shadows" and serves the family's needs for subsistence without jeopardising the role of the feminine role model or the family's ability to care for one another, patriarchal societies may be open to it.

2.2   Global Disruptions and Challenges

The interactions of global trends manifest in complex ways, resulting in novel or multi-layered challenges and opportunities. For example, external shocks, pandemic challenges, climate change challenges the natural environment, and sustainability; emergent technologies can address such challenges. For instance, firms can find new opportunities for innovative products that minimise CO_2 emissions. Repeated external shocks emerging from differentiated sources are posing significant challenges to both multinational enterprises (MNEs) as well as to small and medium firms (SMEs) in a wide variety of sectors and nations. Seventy per cent of all economic sectors globally are directly impacted by extreme weather events like floods and fires brought on by climate change (ibid). The challenges coming from climate change are exacerbated by those coming from the broader complex and ever-changing political and economic scenario, as well as, more recently, from global health-related issues. The impact of tensions on global sourcing and the increasing cost of transport and global procurement have further complicated these trends (World Trade organisation, 2021).

2.2.1 COVID-19 and Emergency Healthcare

Since its start in China in December 2019, the COVID-19 pandemic has had a major impact on every aspect of life, on entrepreneurship and the global economy. The virus's rapid and disruptive spread, coupled with its horrific effects, has eclipsed all previous events. It is spreading to an increasing number of developed, developing, and emerging nations. By March 2020, COVID-19 had been formally designated as a pandemic and as a worldwide health emergency by the World Health Organisation (WHO). The government's attempts to limit the spread of viruses caused massive disruption to entrepreneurship on a social and economic level at various tiers, with small businesses and start-ups being especially affected (Brown & Rocha, 2020). By September 2020, 80% of MNEs' revenue had decreased by 37% as a result of the COVID-19 pandemic's external shock (Saurav et al., 2020). The situation has also been made worse by rising transportation and international procurement costs (World Trade Organisation, 2021). The conversation about how MNEs could be resilient and improve their global value chain (GVC) capability to successfully mitigate such disruptions was given new life by such an undesirable and unexpected crisis (Chatterjee et al., 2024). The COVID-19 pandemic has highlighted the potential weaknesses of global value chains (GVCs), particularly in specific industries and has deepened existing SDG rules, restrictions, and regulations (Zhan, 2021).

Every company on the planet has experienced the pandemic's negative effects. Particularly, because of their inexperience, newly founded and established businesses, start-ups and newly established companies were forced to fire their staff, which led to a decrease in employment, a downturn in the economy, and low productivity.

On the other hand, the COVID-19 pandemic brought about a number of positive changes, like the quick application of innovative solutions which affected entrepreneurship around the globe. For instance, economies have been greatly threatened by COVID-19. In order to deal with the economic downturn, it is essential to preserve economic competitiveness in relation to other nations (He & Harris, 2020). Hence, numerous economies (e.g. China) have developed plans to promote and facilitate entrepreneurship. This healthcare emergency facilitated progress by offering novel business strategies and educational opportunities, and it has also increased the sense of competition among entrepreneurs and established businesses.

2.2.2 Climate Change

As an example of deteriorating Natural Environment and Sustainability, we can mention Climate change, degradation of land, air, and water, Growing scarcity of energy, water, food, and other natural resources, Biodiversity loss, deforestation, and desertification.

As the world grapples with the urgent need for sustainable development, the role of entrepreneurs in driving the transition towards greener economies and societies has never been more critical. Figure 2.1 illustrates the world's ecological deficit and reserves. Corporate entrepreneurship significantly contributes to this category by enabling established companies to innovate and pivot towards more sustainable business practices, products, and services, thereby enhancing their contribution to global sustainability efforts.

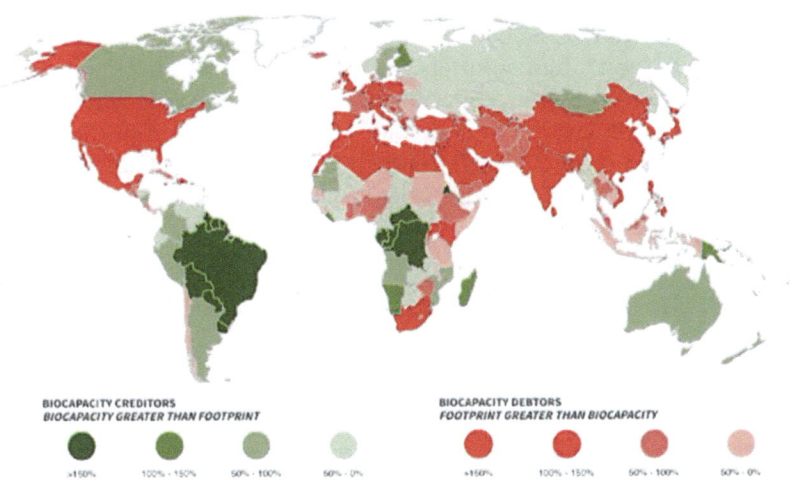

Fig. 2.1 World ecological deficit and reserves. (Source: Global Footprint Network (2023). Data footprint network https://data.footprintnetwork.org/#/)

As factors that influence Sustainability transformation, we can cite home and host country environments (the natural, economic, institutional, regulatory, cultural, social, and market environments in each country), external and internal stakeholders (External: investors, consumers, governments, and society; Internal: owners, managers, employees, and partners). Organisational Environment (Corporate culture, norms, organisational structure, governance system, work environment, types of employees, scale and scope of international activities). Organisational resources (knowledge, capital, human resources, social capital, networks and partners, physical assets, technology, information, data), Organisational Capabilities (Managerial vision, managerial competence, planning ability, innovativeness, technological competence, R&D, capacity for strategic adjustment, partnering abilities, supply chain management, internal processes, controls, analytical skills) Organisational Postures and Strategies (internationalisation strategies, geographic diversification, integration responsiveness, corporate governance, organisational legitimacy, entrepreneurial orientation, market strategies, non-market strategies, communications, disclosure and signalling, philanthropy and activism.

The Earth Overshoot Day, or EOD, is a celebration of the day on which all of humanity has consumed more natural resources than the earth can replenish in a given year. It fell on August 22, 2020. We have 1.7 Earths in use. It fell on July 25, 2024. Because of overfishing, overharvesting of forests, and atmospheric emissions of more carbon dioxide than ecosystems can withstand, humans utilise more ecological resources and services than nature can replenish. This indicator mentions the date when humanity has exhausted nature's budget for the year. For the rest of the year, we are accelerating our ecological deficit by drawing down natural resource stocks. Humanity is now operating in unsustainable "overshoot" on a global level.

2.2.3 Technological Evolution and Artificial Intelligence

Technological evolution with digitalisation and intelligent manufacturing technologies can lead to further challenges for firms and their value chains. For instance, digital technologies are leading to reconfigurations in global value chains (GVCs) because they are capable of modifying the reasons for convenience, the organisational methods, the environmental impact, and the comparison between geographical distance and production and transport costs. This scenario has revived the debate about deploying firms' capabilities and their resilient attitude in responding to external disruptions. The Revolutionary technological advances encompass evolving technological outcomes such as increased connectivity, processing power, digitalisation, and data.

The most recent ground-breaking and emergent technologies include (Quantum computing, Artificial intelligence, Digital platforms, Blockchain, Big data platforms, Smarter tools and analytics, The Internet of Things, Robotics, Autonomous vehicles, Additive manufacturing (3D printing), Nanotechnology, and Biotechnology, Videotelephony, 5G digital cellular networks and Blockchain. The internet has become accessible to a wide range of individuals and firms globally. Figure 2.2 reveals the evolution of the internet users around the world.

Artificial intelligence (AI), first used in the 1950s, is considered the most important technological advancement promoting global digital transformation that can increase human capability at a low cost. It will be the defining technology of the next ten years because disruptive technology has distinctly better qualities than the systems or habits it replaces;

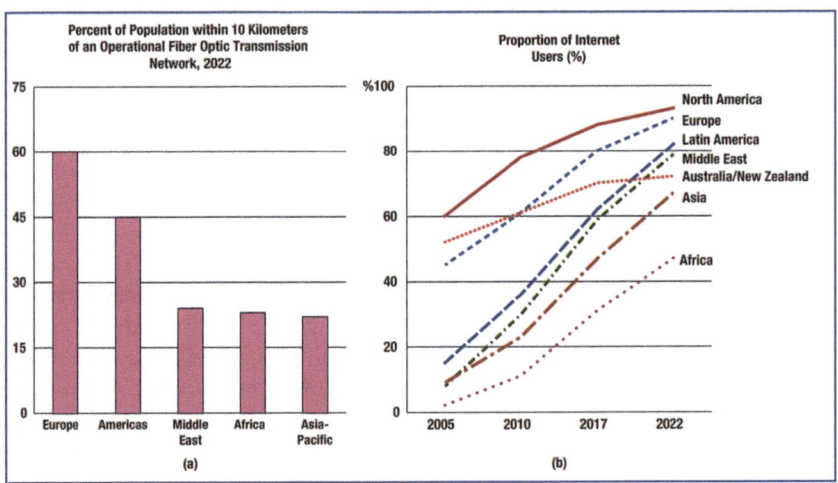

Fig. 2.2 Internet users around the world. (Sources: IMF, World Economic Outlook (Washington, DC: International Monetary Fund, 2023); International Telecommunications Union (2022), Global Connectivity Report 2022, https://www.itu.int/itu-d/reports/statistics/global-connectivityreport-2022/; Internet World Stats, Internet Usage Statistics, 2023, www.internetworldstats.com)

these systems or habits are altered (Akinsola et al., 2022). Big data analytics can now access a vast amount of data thanks to digital transformation.

AI does not have a widely agreed-upon definition. The term artificial intelligence (AI) describes computer programs that are able to carry out sophisticated operations that were previously limited to human performance, such as problem-solving, reasoning, and decision-making. It is commonly known as a machine's capacity for experience-based learning, adaptability to novel inputs, and human-like task performance.

These days, the term "AI" refers to a broad range of technologies that underpin many of the products and services we use on a daily basis, such as chatbots that offer real-time customer support and apps that suggest TV shows. In recent literature, Kelly et al. defined artificial intelligence as "an unnatural object or entity that possesses the ability and capacity to meet or exceed the requirements of the task it is assigned when considering cultural and demographic circumstances" (Kelly et al., 2023, p. 2). They identified three types of artificial intelligence: Artificial General Intelligence (AGI), Artificial Narrow Intelligence (ANI), and Artificial Super Intelligence (ASI). The first type of AI is capable of transferring knowledge across a variety of contexts. The second type of artificial intelligence refers to contemporary AI systems, like Apple's Siri voice recognition software, which helps users through machine learning but is unable to transfer knowledge between tasks or systems. The third type of ASI represents a level of intelligence beyond human comprehension. It has the power to make ground-breaking discoveries in a variety of fields, including general, scientific, academic, artistic, and social, which could eventually render humans redundant (Kelly et al., 2023).

AI is causing disruptive technology, which is being seen in the world today. With the help of this technology, people's daily lives may be improved in a number of ways, including health care (such as surgeries and early tumour detection), education (such as individualised educating aids), transportation (such as automated automobiles), and customer service (such as customised assistants). For instance, in the healthcare industry, in surgery and medicine, artificial intelligence (AI) is becoming more and more popular. AI-based solutions can provide instruments for analysing large amounts of data in order to support complex decision-making processes through predictive analytics (Cobianchi et al., 2023).

In fact, the relationship between businesses, employees, and customers has evolved fundamentally as a result of the rapid growth and widespread application of artificial intelligence (AI) and other ground-breaking technologies. Therefore, the field of human resource management is currently undergoing a global revolution and transformation due to the rapid advancement of innovative technologies (Vrontis et al., 2023).

2.3 GLOBAL TRANSFORMATION

The business world has undergone a global transformation as a result of the previously mentioned global disruptions, primarily in the areas of digital transformation, sustainable transformation, and social transformation.

2.3.1 Digital Transformation

Regardless of the industry they operate in, digital transformation has become essential for the majority of organisations. According to Westerman et al. (2014), "digital transformation" is typically understood to be the application of innovation and new digital technologies to improve an organisation's business operations. We have witnessed something in recent years that goes far beyond "business improvements" brought about by the simple use of IT solutions. According to Gong and Ribiere (2021) and Merín-Rodrigáñez et al. (2024), digital transformation (DT) is a massive revolution that is bringing about new ways of conceptualising innovation itself through new skills, new business models and disruptive ways of executing exponential change within organisations. As it significantly impacts corporate architecture, core competencies, and frequently the company's purpose, it is, in fact, a true "transformation". Table 2.1 summarises some definitions of digital transformations.

Digital transformation is now an irreversible force that shapes the organ of organisations and strategies in the global business environment. This transformational change, integral to the Fourth Industrial Revolution, marks a radical shift in organisational engagement with technology, data, and digital processes to change at core their operations, value propositions, and the very essence of competitive advantage. Revolution attributes a combination of technologies that blur the lines between physical, digital, and biological driving, from rapid progress in artificial intelligence, robotics, the Internet of Things (IoT), autonomous vehicles, 3D printing, and quantum computing. None of these technologies really promise to revolutionise the industries; they challenge traditional models of management and operation and keep urging organisations around the world to adapt very quickly in order not to be toppled out of relevance and

Table 2.1 Some definitions of digital transformation

Authors	Definition of digital transformation
Westerman et al. (2011)	The use of technology to radically improve the performance or reach of the enterprise.
Westerman et al. (2014)	The implementation of innovation and new digital technologies to effect business improvements in an organisation.
Bekkhus (2016)	The use of digital technologies to radically improve the company's performance.
Gruman (2016)	The application of digital technologies fundamentally impacts all aspects of business and society.
Fitzgerald et al. (2014)	The use of new digital technologies (social media, mobile, analytics or embedded devices) to enable major business improvements (such as enhancing customer experience, streamlining operations or creating new business models).
Brown et al. (2014)	Encompassing everything from the cultural and organisational changes required to the related use of new digital technologies in order to enable major improvements—such as enhancing user services, streamlining operations or creating entirely new services.
Horlacher (2016)	Digital technology is used to enable major business improvements in operations and the market, such as enhancing customer experience, streamlining operations, or creating new business models.

Source: Adapted from (Gong & Ribiere, 2021)

competitiveness. At the very core of this paradigmatic shift is the notion of digital transformation: moving from the adoption of technology to the full-scale cultural, process, and strategy change of an organisation. It includes the rethinking of old operation models, experimentation with new business approaches, and a culture that can innovate with agility and constant learning. It is a complex, multifaceted process touching every part of an organisation and demanding a comprehensive, coordinated approach to change management.

The digital transformation opportunities, among others, can be (1) Rising demand for cutting-edge products and services featuring new technologies, (2) Smart use of technology increases connectivity, innovation, productivity, and control over value chain activities, (3) Smart use of technology optimises management, marketing, finance, and other business functions.

For instance, The innovative technologies mentioned above support SMEs through their ability to facilitate the efficient and cost-effective realisation of sustainability initiatives, overcoming the liabilities of small size, externalisation of value chain activities, and foreignness. These technologies have very low costs of transmitting data and information worldwide and of transacting with customers and value-chain partners, they have greater efficiency in and control of value-chain activities, greater ability to innovate, greater ability to collaborate, and increased capacity to automate many sustainability-related activities, e.g., monitoring pollution and waste, which help to address sustainability. Therefore, businesses may gain a competitive edge and enjoy the benefits of emerging technologies as a result of digital transformation (Warner & Wäger, 2019). By developing new products that are faster, smarter, more connected, and perform better, DT enables businesses to expand the value of their product line (Porter & Heppelmann, 2014). Moreover, DT enables businesses to develop intangible digital offerings, like apps, that are distributed via digital infrastructure (Monaghan et al., 2020). Digitalised organisations can instantly and inexpensively access markets by using digital channels to provide services and communicate with clients (Stallkamp & Schotter, 2021). But for many businesses, putting DT into practice and then enjoying its advantages is a difficult task (Giustiziero et al., 2023; Merín-Rodrigáñez et al., 2024).

However, it is noted that the digital transformation and the revolutionary technological advances have some threats that include the following: (1) disparity of technology access in large parts of the world; (2) insufficient skills in firms and individuals to manage novel technologies. (3) job loss arising from automation, robotics, and artificial intelligence.

2.3.2 Sustainable Transformation

Sustainability is about Meeting humanity's needs today without harming the ability of future generations to meet their needs. It is related to Corporate Social Performance—principles, practices, and outcomes of company relationships with people, organisations, institutions, communities, societies, and the earth, as deliberate actions directed to stakeholders and the unintended externalities of business activity, and to the 'triple bottom line approach'—economic, environmental, and social. The society and people encompass Human rights, social inclusion, equity, poverty, energy access, health & well-being, and working conditions. The economy and profit include Economic & financial viability, Environmental profit and Societal profit. The environment and planet include Deforestation & biodiversity loss, Water scarcity & sanitation, Waste,

Natural resource depletion, Land pollution, Water pollution, Air pollution, and Climate change.

Sustainability conditions and needs differ by industry. For example, the most polluting industries are energy, transportation, retailing, manufacturing, agriculture, and fashion. Sustainability has been identified as a major concern on a global scale (Wang et al., 2019).

'Sustainable transformation' is the process of implementing significant changes to practices, systems, and behaviours in a way that satisfies current needs without compromising the capacity of future generations to satisfy their own needs. The fundamental basis of this notion is sustainability, which maintains the long-term viability and well-being of our planet and its people by balancing environmental, social, and economic factors. Walker et al. (2004) defined sustainability transformations as shifts that essentially change the interactions and feedback between humans and the environment.

There are several domains in which sustainable transformation can take place, including environmental, which involves modifying the use and management of resources to stop their depletion and degradation. This entails using energy-efficient techniques, switching to renewable energy sources, and implementing sustainable manufacturing and agriculture methods. Social: improving people's quality of life and guaranteeing fairness and resource access for all. Promoting social justice, inclusivity, and community resilience are all part of this. Economic: adapting economic frameworks to encourage sustainable practices; examples include creating circular economies, which reduce waste and reuse materials, and supporting environmentally friendly businesses and technologies. Cultural: Modifying consumer behaviour, encouraging sustainable living, and cultivating respect for the environment are all examples of altering cultural norms and values to support sustainability practices.

Sustainability entrepreneurship, within the realm of international entrepreneurship, centres on the establishment of companies that prioritise social and environmental responsibility with a clear international dimension. By implementing eco-friendly practices and advocating sustainable consumption and production, these ventures address global sustainability issues. Noteworthy research by Schaltegger et al. (2016) underscores the global significance of sustainability entrepreneurship in promoting environmental stewardship and international resilience.

Koe et al. (2014) identified four drivers for the propensity of sustainable entrepreneurship. Those four drivers are the *sustainable attitude* of the entrepreneurial actor, *social norms* (the social pressure to act in an environmentally responsible manner), *perceived desirability* (an individual's sensitivity toward the attractiveness of a behaviour), and *perceived feasibility* (an individual's perfection about his/her capabilities and self-efficacy). Recent years have witnessed a growing stream of entrepreneurship linked to sustainability in developing and manufacturing their products. For instance, many entrepreneurs have included sustainability principles in their company's strategy. Others follow a waste minimisation practice and use natural fabrics in their products (Fletcher, 2013; Henninger et al., 2016). These entrepreneurs, while attempting not to harm the world and pollute the environment, have paid particular attention to product quality and human health (Akarslan & Demiralay, 2015).

In addition to discussing sustainability, it's critical to bring up the phenomenon of "greenwashing." Growing environmental problems like increasing air pollution, declining food security, and pollution from waste disposal have forced many businesses worldwide to focus more on the sustainability issue. Furthermore, these issues increased public awareness of environmental issues and put more pressure on businesses to disclose their environmental impact and provide eco-friendly products. Customers may be more willing to pay more for products from companies they believe to be socially conscious if they believe these companies operate in a responsible manner. This could result in the "Greenwashing" phenomenon, which is the dissemination of false information to convince customers that a company is environmentally friendly, sustainable, or biodegradable. The environmentalist Jay Westervelt first used the term "greenwashing" in 1986 when hotels started requesting that guests reuse their towels. They claimed that this was a water-saving tactic, but they were not taking any other environmental measures that would address more serious environmental problems.

Webster's New Millennium Dictionary of English describes this phenomenon as the "practice of promoting environmentally friendly programs to deflect attention from an organisation's environmentally unfriendly or less savoury activities." This definition is supported by a number of dictionaries. "Poor environmental performance and positive communication about environmental performance" are the definitions of "greenwashing" given by Delmas and Burbano. (Delmas & Burbano, 2011, p. 2). The act of providing false information to customers about a company's environmental policies or the advantages of a product or service for the environment is known as "greenwashing".

The evolution of technologies helps firms, as they can Reduce energy usage, waste, pollution, the use of natural resources, the need for long-distance transportation, the need for extensive supply chains and distribution channels, increase productivity, social inclusion, diversity, access to social goods (such as healthcare and education), the ability to optimise sourcing and distribution, work environment safety and superior working conditions, generally rationalise company operations, which saves energy, reduces pollution, and may improve working conditions, and Save resources that can be applied to support sustainability.

2.3.3 Social Transformation

Rabie (2013) defined social transformation as 'Social transformation means the restructuring of all aspects of life; from culture to social relations; from politics to economy; from the way we think to the way we live' (ibid., p. 59). Social transformation can refer to the process by which war, political upheaval, scientific advancements, economic growth, and technological innovations cause society to change. Small associations of people bound by instincts, need, and fear have given way to small communities bound by circumstances, kinship, traditions, and religious beliefs; these communities have then developed into nations bound by politics, ideology, culture, laws, history, and other factors.

Migration is an essential and inevitable component of the larger processes of social transformation that characterise societies undergoing "modernisation." The United Nations defined the international migrant as 'any person who has changed his or her country of residence, including all migrants, regardless of their legal status, or the nature, or motive of their movement' (UN DESA, 1980). Others have defined a second-generation migration topic. For instance, the Migration and Home Affairs website of the European Commission defined a second-generation migrant as "A person who was born in and is residing in a country that at least one of their parents previously entered as a migrant".

While specific migration patterns and levels vary amongst societies, significant increases in overall levels of internal and global movement are usually the result of a confluence of profound economic, cultural, technological, political, and demographic transitions (De Haas, 2020). According to (De Haas, 2021), migration is a social process that is inextricably linked to larger processes of change of which it is a component. Additionally, the author conceptualised migration as an integral component of larger processes of demographic, technological, cultural, political, and economic change, as evidenced by terms like "development," "social transformation," and globalisation.

The emergence of migrant entrepreneurship in this intricate scenario proves to be a powerful force for economic growth and social inclusion. An important destination for the growing migrations from South Africa, the Middle and Far East, and Latin America is Europe. 2.3 million immigrants from outside the EU entered the EU in 2021, while 1.4 million citizens of one EU member state moved to another (Eurostat, 2023). Following the end of the pandemic, the aforementioned data witnessed a sharp increase. These data demonstrate how these flows are altering European society and how migration is a complex phenomenon that involves both internal migration and external migration, with people arriving in Europe from all over the world. Figure 2.3 illustrates the evolution of global migration in the last few years.

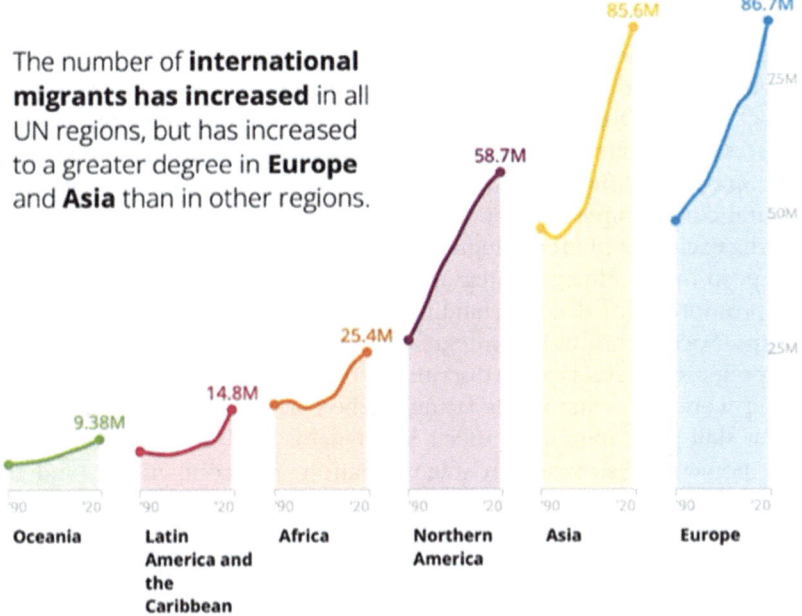

Fig. 2.3 The evolution of global migration in the last years. (Source: UN DESA, 2021)

According to the United Nations, in 2020, there were an estimated 281 million international migrants worldwide (International Organization for Migration, 2020). Women migrants comprise 48% of all international migrants (United Nations, 2019), making the case for female transnational entrepreneurship highly relevant (Lee & Lee, 2020; Ratten & Pellegrini, 2020). According to current estimates, there were approximately 281 million international migrants worldwide in 2020, accounting for 3.6% of the world's population and more than three times the estimated number from 1970 (IOM, 2023). The phenomenon is likely to persist and intensify, especially if problems like poverty, inequality, war, and climate change are not adequately addressed. Female migrant entrepreneurship, defined as 'Undertaking entrepreneurial activities, in particular creating new businesses by first or second-generation immigrants' (Christensen et al., 2020), became a hot topic that has emerged recently in the context of increasing the number of female migration globally, especially from developing-to-developed countries, (Kabbara et al., 2025; Chreim et al., 2018).

Migration processes have a social transformation impact on and change local, national, and international societies, cultures, economies, and institutions. Whether it is voluntary or forced, migration has a significant social impact and can change society in both positive and negative ways. Local cultures are enriched and transformed as a result of the frequent migration of people from different cultural backgrounds. As a result, thriving multicultural communities may be formed, as well as new cultural hybridities and the exchange of ideas, languages, and customs. Social cohesion can be enhanced by the effective integration of migrants into host societies, as it can promote mutual understanding, empathy, and unity among diverse groups. Social tensions and integration efforts can be hampered by issues like prejudice, stereotyping, discrimination, and social exclusion. By providing workers for industries facing a labour shortage and bridging particular skill gaps, migration affects the dynamics of the labour market. It may, however, also result in wage deflation, job competition, and the exploitation of migrant labourers, particularly those with unauthorised or irregular status. Migration contributes to demographic transformations by altering population composition, which has a big impact on social welfare programmes, healthcare, education, and pension systems.

Migrants, particularly women, confront multi-layered liabilities" during their entrepreneurial endeavours in the host country, encompassing the liability of foreignness, origin, gender, newness, and smallness. These layered liabilities affect both the individual, including their comprehension and perception of the host context and how the context perceives them and the firm as being small and new in a foreign context. Additionally, these liabilities extend to the network, as migrants often find themselves as outsiders in the host context, both socially and within interorganisational networks. In addition to their place of origin, migrants can be identified by the reasons behind their migration. While some are economic migrants looking for better opportunities, others are refugees fleeing persecution. The different conditions that surround migration have an impact on a number of things, most notably the creation of a new venture, which is the main topic of this book. Several obstacles may be imposed by the institutions that support entrepreneurship among immigrants and refugees. European nations differ greatly from one another, and this is mirrored in both their immigration laws and the sentiments of their populace towards immigrants.

References

Akarslan, F., & Demiralay, H. (2015). Effects of textile materials harmful to human health. *Acta Physica Polonica A, 128*(2B), 407–409.

Akinsola, J., Adeagbo, M., Oladapo, K., Akinsehinde, S., & Onipede, F. (2022). Artificial intelligence emergence in disruptive technology. In *Computational intelligence and data sciences* (pp. 63–90). CRC Press.

Bekkhus, R. (2016). *Do KPIs used by CIOs decelerate digital business transformation?* The case of ITIL.

Blackburn, R., & Smallbone, D. (2014). Sustaining self-employment for disadvantaged entrepreneurs.

Bonnet, F., Vanek, J., & Chen, M. (2019). *Women and men in the informal economy: A statistical brief* (p. 20). International Labour Office.

Brown, A., Fishenden, J., Thompson, M., Brown, A., Fishenden, J., & Thompson, M. (2014). Organizational structures and digital transformation. In *Digitizing government: Understanding and implementing new digital business models* (pp. 165–183).

Brown, R., & Rocha, A. (2020). Entrepreneurial uncertainty during the Covid-19 crisis: Mapping the temporal dynamics of entrepreneurial finance. *Journal of Business Venturing Insights, 14*, e00174.

Canelas, C. (2019). Informality and poverty in Ecuador. *Small Business Economics, 53*, 1097–1115.

Castro, I. A., Swayne, M. R., Lowery, B. C., & Gonzalez, G. R. (2024). Societal transformation through social entrepreneurial action research. *Journal of Public Policy & Marketing*, 07439156241236769.

Chatterjee, S., Chaudhuri, R., Vrontis, D., Dana, L.-P., & Kabbara, D. (2024). Developing resilience of MNEs: From global value chain (GVC) capability and performance perspectives. *Journal of Business Research, 172*, 114447.

Chreim, S., Spence, M., Crick, D., & Liao, X. L. (2018). Review of female immigrant entrepreneurship research: Past findings, gaps and ways forward. *European Management Journal, 36*(2), 210–222.

Christensen, L. J., Newman, A. B., Herrick, H., & Godfrey, P. (2020). Separate but not equal: Toward a nomological net for migrants and migrant entrepreneurship. *Journal of International Business Policy, 3*(1), 1–22.

Cobianchi, L., Piccolo, D., Dal Mas, F., Agnoletti, V., Ansaloni, L., Balch, J., et al. (2023). Surgeons' perspectives on artificial intelligence to support clinical decision-making in trauma and emergency contexts: Results from an international survey. *World Journal of Emergency Surgery, 18*(1), 1.

De Haas, H. (2020). Paradoxes of migration and development. In *Routledge handbook of migration and development* (pp. 17–31). Routledge.

De Haas, H. (2021). A theory of migration: The aspirations-capabilities framework. *Comparative Migration Studies, 9*(1), 8.

Delmas, M. A., & Burbano, V. C. (2011). The drivers of greenwashing. *California Management Review, 54*(1), 64–87.

Eurostat. (2023). Migration and migrant population statistics. https://ec.europa.eu/eurostat/statistics-explained/index.php?title=Migration_and_migrant_population_statistics&stable=1

Fairlie, R. W., & Fossen, F. M. (2018). Opportunity versus necessity entrepreneurship: Two components of business creation.

Fitzgerald, M., Kruschwitz, N., Bonnet, D., & Welch, M. (2014). Embracing digital technology: A new strategic imperative. *MIT Sloan Management Review, 55*(2), 1.

Fletcher, K. (2013). *Sustainable fashion and textiles: Design journeys*. Routledge.

Formica, P. (2023). Transformative entrepreneurship. In *The Palgrave encyclopedia of entrepreneurship* (pp. 1–11). Springer.

Giraldo, M., Garcia-Tello, L., & Rayburn, S. W. (2020). Street vending: Transformative entrepreneurship for individual and collective well-being. *Journal of Services Marketing, 34*(6), 757–768.

Giustiziero, G., Kretschmer, T., Somaya, D., et al. (2023). Hyperspecialization and hyperscaling: A resource-based theory of the digital firm. *Strategic Management Journal 44*(6), 1391–1424.

Global Footprint Network. (2023). *Advancing the Science of Sustainability*. Retrieved online on 21 July 2024 at https://data.footprintnetwork.org/#/

Gong, C., & Ribiere, V. (2021). Developing a unified definition of digital transformation. *Technovation, 102*, 102217.

Gruman, G. (2016). What digital transformation really means. *InfoWorld, 18*(1), 1–3.

Günther, I., & Launov, A. (2012). Informal employment in developing countries: Opportunity or last resort? *Journal of Development Economics, 97*(1), 88–98.

Harati, R. (2013). Heterogeneity in the Egyptian informal labour market: Choice or obligation? *Revue d'économie politique, 4*, 623–639.

Harris, J. A. (2012). *Transformative entrepreneurs: How Walt Disney, Steve Jobs, Muhammad Yunus, and other innovators succeeded*. Springer.

He, H., & Harris, L. (2020). The impact of Covid-19 pandemic on corporate social responsibility and marketing philosophy. *Journal of Business Research, 116*, 176–182.

Hearle, C., Baden, S., & Kalsi, K. (2019). Promoting economic empowerment for women in the informal economy. *WOW helpdesk guidance no, 1*.

Henninger, C. E., Alevizou, P. J., & Oates, C. J. (2016). What is sustainable fashion? *Journal of Fashion Marketing and Management: An International Journal*.

Horlacher, A. (2016). Co-creating value – The dyadic CDO-CIO relationship during the digital transformation.

International Organization for Migration, U. N. (2020). *World migration report*. International Organization for Migration.

IOM. (2023). International Office for Migration), United Nations, World Migration Report. UN.

Kabbara, D. (2023). Female entrepreneurship: Typologies, drivers and value creation. In *New horizons and global perspectives in female entrepreneurship research* (pp. 93–112). Emerald Publishing Limited.

Kabbara, D., Suárez-Ortega, S. M., & Zucchella, A. (2025). Developing entrepreneurial opportunities through multi-layered liabilities: the experiences of female migrant entrepreneurs. *The International Entrepreneurship and Management Journal, 21*(1), 1–32, https://doi.org/10.1007/s11365-024-01010-3.

Kelly, S., Kaye, S.-A., & Oviedo-Trespalacios, O. (2023). What factors contribute to the acceptance of artificial intelligence? A systematic review. *Telematics and Informatics, 77*, 101925.

Koe, W.-L., Omar, R., & Majid, I. A. (2014). Factors associated with propensity for sustainable entrepreneurship. *Procedia-Social and Behavioral Sciences, 130*, 65–74.

Kogut, C. S., & Mejri, K. (2021). Female entrepreneurship in emerging markets: Challenges of running a business in turbulent contexts and times. *International Journal of Gender and Entrepreneurship*.

Lee, J. Y., & Lee, J. Y. (2020). Female Transnational Entrepreneurs (FTEs): A case study of Korean American female entrepreneurs in Silicon Valley. *Journal of Entrepreneurship and Innovation in Emerging Economies, 6*(1), 67–83.

Madelin, R., & Ringrose, D. (2016). *Opportunity Now: Europe's Mission to Innovate*. The Publications Office of the European Union.

Merín-Rodrigáñez, J., Dasí, À., & Alegre, J. (2024). Digital transformation and firm performance in innovative SMEs: The mediating role of business model innovation. *Technovation 134*, 103027.

Miller, R. A., & Collier, E. W. (2010). Redefining entrepreneurship: A virtues and values perspective. *Journal of Leadership, Accountability and Ethics, 8*(2), 80–89.

Monaghan, S., Tippmann, E., & Coviello, N. (2020). Born digitals: Thoughts on their internationalization and a research agenda. *Journal of International Business Studies 51*(1), 11–22.

OECD/The European Commission. (2013). The Missing Entrepreneurs: Policies for Inclusive Entrepreneurship in Europe, OECD Publishing., https://doi.org/10.1787/9789264188167-en.

OECD/The European Commission. (2014). *The Missing Entrepreneurs: Policies for Inclusive Entrepreneurship in Europe*, OECD Publishing. https://doi.org/10.1787/9789264213593-en.

OECD/European Union. (2015). The Missing Entrepreneurs 2015: Policies for Self-employment and Entrepreneurship, OECD Publishing, Paris. https://doi.org/10.1787/9789264226418-en.

Porter, ME., & Heppelmann, JE. (2014). How smart, connected products are transforming competition. *Harvard business review 92*(11), 64–88.

Rabie, M. (2013). Social transformation. In M. Rabie (Ed.), *Global economic and cultural transformation: The making of history* (pp. 59–77). Palgrave Macmillan US.

Ratten, V., & Jones, P. (2018). Transformational entrepreneurship: An overview. *Transformational entrepreneurship*, 1–17.

Ratten, V., & Pellegrini, M. M. (2020). Female transnational entrepreneurship and smart specialization policy. *Journal of Small Business & Entrepreneurship, 32*(6), 545–566.

Salvi, E., Belz, F.-M., & Bacq, S. (2023). Informal entrepreneurship: An integrative review and future research agenda. *Entrepreneurship Theory and Practice, 47*(2), 265–303.

Saurav, A., Kusek, P., Kuo, R., & Viney, B. (2020). *The impact of COVID-19 on foreign investors*. World Bank Publications.

Schaltegger, S., Lüdeke-Freund, F., & Hansen, E. G. (2016). Business models for sustainability: A co-evolutionary analysis of sustainable entrepreneurship, innovation, and transformation. *Organization & Environment, 29*(3), 264–289. https://doi.org/10.1177/1086026616633272.

Stallkamp, M., & Schotter, AP. (2021). Platforms without borders? The international strategies of digital platform firms. *Global Strategy Journal 11*(1), 58–80.

Teece, D. J. (2018). Profiting from innovation in the digital economy: Enabling technologies, standards, and licensing models in the wireless world. *Research Policy, 47*(8), 1367–1387.

UN DESA. (1980). Recommendations on statistics of international migration (Statistical Papers, Serie M, No. 58, Rev.1). *Department of Economic and Social Affairs, Statistic Division*. Retrieved from https://unstats.un.org/unsd/publication/seriesm/seriesm_58rev1e.pdf

UN DESA. (2021). United nations Department of Economic and Social Affairs, Statistic Division, retrieved online on 19 June 2024 from https://worldmigrationreport.iom.int/msite/wmr-2024-interactive/.

UNDP. (2022). Data future exchange 'Informal Economy Data Explorer'. Retrieved December 11, 2023, from https://data.undp.org/insights/informal-economy

United Nations, D. o. E. a. S. A., Population Division. (2019). International Migration 2019: Wall Chart (ST/ESA/SER/A/431).

Vrontis, D., Christofi, M., Pereira, V., Tarba, S., Makrides, A., & Trichina, E. (2023). Artificial intelligence, robotics, advanced technologies and human resource management: A systematic review. *Artificial Intelligence and International HRM*, 172–201.

Walker, B., Holling, C. S., Carpenter, S. R., & Kinzig, A. (2004). Resilience, adaptability and transformability in social–ecological systems. *Ecology and Society, 9*(2).

Wang, H., Liu, H., Kim, S. J., & Kim, K. H. (2019). Sustainable fashion index model and its implication. *Journal of Business Research, 99*, 430–437.

Warner, K. S., & Wäger, M. (2019). Building dynamic capabilities for digital transformation: An ongoing process of strategic renewal. *Long Range Planning, 52*(3), 326–349.

Webb, J. W., Khoury, T. A., & Hitt, M. A. (2020). The influence of formal and informal institutional voids on entrepreneurship. *Entrepreneurship Theory and Practice, 44*(3), 504–526.

Welter, F., Smallbone, D., & Pobol, A. (2015). Entrepreneurial activity in the informal economy: A missing piece of the entrepreneurship jigsaw puzzle. *Entrepreneurship & Regional Development, 27*(5–6), 292–306.

Westerman, G., Bonnet, D., & McAfee, A. (2014). *Leading digital: Turning technology into business transformation*. Harvard Business Press.

Westerman, G., Calméjane, C., Bonnet, D., Ferraris, P., & McAfee, A. (2011). Digital transformation: A roadmap for billion-dollar organizations. *MIT Center for digital business and capgemini consulting, 1*, 1–68.

WorldBank. (2019). Female entrepreneurship resource point – Introduction and module 1: Why gender matters. Retrieved December 14, 2019, from www.worldbank.org/en/topic/gender/publication/female-entrepreneurship-resource-point-introduction-and-module-1-why-gender-matters

World Trade Organization. (2021). World Trade Report 2021: Economic resilience and trade retrieved online January, 31st, 2022 at https://www.wto.org/english/res_e/booksp_e/wtr21_e/00_wtr21_e.pdf

Xheneti, M., Madden, A., & Thapa Karki, S. (2019). Value of formalization for women entrepreneurs in developing contexts: A review and research agenda. *International Journal of Management Reviews, 21*(1), 3–23.

Zhan, J. X. (2021). GVC transformation and a new investment landscape in the 2020s: Driving forces, directions, and a forward-looking research and policy agenda. *Journal of International Business Policy, 4*(2), 206–220.

CHAPTER 3

Global Female Entrepreneurship: Exploring The Motivations and Challenges

Abstract In light of the recent global disruption and the increasing prominence of digital technologies, internationalisation is regarded as a critical path for business growth and as a primary force behind agile market expansion for both established enterprises and start-up ventures. Transformative international entrepreneurship represents a dynamic approach to female business that prioritises positive social, economic, and environmental change over mere profit maximisation. This paradigm shift underscores the importance of value-driven business practices and the pivotal role of visionary female international entrepreneurs in driving international business and sustainable development. This chapter will address the evolution of the international process of the companies, from born global firms to the rise of the Unicorns start-ups and illustrate the main factors that affect the high international growth of these firms. This chapter also highlights the motivation and challenges faced by female international entrepreneurs. The chapter concludes with a case study about 'Huda Kattan Beauty' as a successful American global female entrepreneur in the cosmetic industry.

Keywords Transformative international entrepreneurship • Born global firms • Unicorns start-ups • Female international entrepreneurs • Challenges • Motivation

© The Author(s), under exclusive license to Springer Nature Switzerland AG 2025
D. Kabbara, *Transformative Entrepreneurship in the Global Landscape*, https://doi.org/10.1007/978-3-031-77141-5_3

3.1 Global Female Entrepreneurship

The field of international entrepreneuship encompasses "diverse organisations, different levels of analysis (individuals, teams, their organisations, networks and -more recently- platforms and ecosystems), different research foci (internationalisation process versus comparative studies in entrepreneurship)" (Zucchella, 2021, p. 7). International female entrepreneurship is an important category of transformative entrepreneurship that focuses on the role of women in founding businesses that drive social and economic transformation on both a domestic and international scale. Greater representation of women in diverse industries and the emergence of innovative ideas are key elements of international entrepreneurship's transformative potential. Notable research by (Brush et al., 2019) goes into the depths of the motivations, challenges, and impacts of female entrepreneurs in international contexts, emphasising their revolutionary potential. International entrepreneurship scholars have recently devoted increasing attention to female exploration and exploitation of international opportunities. The term exploration involves "search, variation, risk-taking, experimentation, play, flexibility, discovery and innovation", while exploitation includes "refinement, choice, production, efficiency, selection, implementation, and execution" (March, 1991, p. 71).

The increasing visibility and success of female entrepreneurs on the global stage signify a promising shift towards greater gender equality and empowerment in the entrepreneurial sphere. Corporate entrepreneurship offers avenues for empowering female intrapreneurs, providing them with the resources and platform to lead transformative projects within established organisations. This support not only enhances the impact of female-led initiatives but also promotes gender equality and empowerment in the corporate world, aligning with broader goals of transformative international entrepreneurship. With the aid of these technologies, women can break through conventional barriers, promote ongoing innovation, and improve operational efficiency in their companies. Digital strategies also improve visibility and connectivity, which empowers female entrepreneurs to drive transformative change across industries and establish global networks.

3.1.1 Entrepreneurial Endeavours

Existing female entrepreneurship research has underlined the crucial role of female entrepreneurs' networks in their entrepreneurial endeavours (Manello et al., 2020; McAdam et al., 2019; Munkejord, 2017). Networks refer to the relationship between the entrepreneur and other organisations and individuals in the broader environment (Kabbara & Zucchella, 2013). Female entrepreneurs may rely on private and business contacts to acquire information and tangible resources (capital, skills) (Munkejord, 2017) that are difficult to obtain in the market or to enhance their internationalisation process (Zucchella & Kabbara, 2013). These resources will enable the achievement of the female entrepreneur's aims. Several types of networks were recognised as crucial in the literature on female entrepreneurship. Many authors identified how border-spanning networks based on family ties (Arregle et al., 2015; Ezzedeen & Zikic, 2017; Mustafa & Chen, 2010), business ties (Munkejord, 2017), community ties (Chrysostome & Lin, 2010), and ethnic ties (Pruthi et al., 2018) enable female entrepreneurs to participate in entrepreneurial activities. These ties are considered social capital and are recognised as an essential component of the female entrepreneurial network (McAdam et al., 2019).

The female entrepreneurship literature stressed the role of the female entrepreneur's family as an important source of network ties in which entrepreneurs can be embedded in "family embeddedness" (Aldrich & Cliff, 2003). In particular, the family members, especially partners, help the female entrepreneur to set up individual businesses (Discua Cruz et al., 2013). For instance, all female entrepreneurs (immigrant, digital, sustainable, resilient) rely on family social ties to acquire valuable resources through family network ties. Family ties have distinctive characteristics resulting in a particular type of social capital (Arregle et al., 2015) which are vital to undertaking entrepreneurial activities (Discua Cruz et al., 2013; Munkejord, 2017). As a female and mother entrepreneur, managing work and family responsibilities is one of the major challenges women face (Rey-Martí et al., 2015; Wu et al., 2019). Hence, family ties deliver balancing work and family (Agarwal & Lenka, 2015; Rehman & Roomi, 2012). Additionally, it provides emotional support, which generates emotional stability and psychic resources (Arregle et al., 2015) and helps the female entrepreneur by increasing motivation, commitment, and confidence (Rehman & Roomi, 2012). In addition to providing these resources, family social ties can provide a tangible source of capital and ready access to business resources (Ezzedeen & Zikic, 2017). The latter can be delivered not only as patient financial capital (Brush et al., 2009), which does not require repayment in the short term, but also as physical capital (equipment) and labour (Aldrich & Cliff, 2003). Moreover, family ties also provide organisational skills and knowledge (Mustafa & Chen, 2010), allowing the female entrepreneur to access business advice characterised by high quality and rapidity at low cost. The Internet and technology enable the female entrepreneur to network with their actors.

Their network became a combination of global and local connectivity; their social relations became more geographically dispersed because of technological advancements. Through blogs and digital media, online communication facilitates long-distance social networks and helps them to cross national boundaries without actual bodily movement (Jafari-Sadeghi et al., 2021).

Additionally, according to (Sussan & Acs, 2017), the Internet has emerged as a potent instrument for initiating new business ventures and boosting operational effectiveness. It could lower entry barriers into international entrepreneurship and provide a wealth of knowledge and information. Therefore, women who encounter obstacles when pursuing global entrepreneurship can greatly benefit from technology (Crittenden et al., 2019).

3.1.2 Empowering Diversity and Equity in Female Entrepreneurship Globally

Gender plays a significant role in the entrepreneurial process; female entrepreneurship has become an interesting field of research and practice, as females are changing cultures and creating wealth for their countries (Díaz-García & Jiménez-Moreno, 2010; Kobeissi, 2010).

According to the Global Entrepreneurship Monitor 2018/2019 Report on Women's Entrepreneurship, 252 million women around the world are entrepreneurs, with another 153 million managing established firms (Hechavarria et al., 2017). Given the importance of women entrepreneurs in improving the quality of life, their role was studied in several entrepreneurship areas.

The number of women entrepreneurs is continuously growing and an estimated 252 million women set up or run a business worldwide (Global Entrepreneurship Monitor, 2023). Nevertheless, Europe still shows gaps between female and male entrepreneurs, and the share of female entrepreneurs is constantly below the men's share. More than half of the European population is female, but only 30% of start-ups are founded by women.

Being the fastest-growing type of entrepreneurship, female entrepreneurs have gained increased attention in the literature over the last few years. The first academic paper on female entrepreneurship was published by Schwartz in 1976 and other authors have since then addressed the topic. Kamala Singh (as cited in Jakhar & Krishna, 2020, p. 38) defines a female entrepreneur as "a confident, innovative and creative woman capable of achieving economic independence individually or in collaboration generates employment opportunities for others through initiating establishing and running an enterprise by keeping pace with her personal, family and social life." Onyusheva and Meyer (2020, p. 265) describe the female entrepreneurs as "the bearer of new thinking, philosophy, lifestyle, value attitudes and morality."

Previous studies reveal that women significantly enhance entrepreneurial activity and drive economic development while feeding their markets, bringing new insights, ideas and innovations. Women contribute substantially to creating new jobs and boosting the gross domestic product (GDP), a view supported by (Ribes-Giner et al., 2018). This impact goes beyond economic growth; it also helps to reduce poverty and social exclusion (Dean et al., 2019). Throughout the world, the involvement of women in entrepreneurship plays a crucial role in promoting stability, enhancing the welfare of communities, and offering economic opportunities for disadvantaged populations such as women, individuals with low incomes, and minority groups (Ascher, 2012).

Onyusheva and Meyer (2020) identified three groups of female entrepreneurs. The first group, which makes up the biggest part, is motivated by the inner desire and free will to become an entrepreneur. The second group is influenced by unexpected circumstances and is entering the business occasionally. The third group, which is the smallest, did involuntarily become entrepreneurs through unfavourable circumstances like unemployment or external pressure.

Ascher (2012) derived a typology of profiles of female entrepreneurs from the research by Bruni et al. (2004). Young women entering entrepreneurship due to unemployment are termed "Aimless." Those who see entrepreneurship as a long-term strategy are described as "Success oriented." "Strongly success-oriented" women view entrepreneurship as a path to self-fulfilment, while "Dualists" seek flexibility to balance family and professional responsibilities. "Return workers" are women who left their jobs for family duties and now seek fulfilment outside the home. "Traditionalists" have a strong family tradition in entrepreneurship. Lastly, Radicals" aim to introduce more pro-female tendencies in society. It is important to note that women entrepreneurs are noted for their risk-taking abilities in managing business uncertainties confidently and effectively. Organisational skills are another significant characteristic, as women entrepreneurs efficiently organise work and people, minimising losses and reducing production costs. Their foresight allows them to foresee future market and technological changes, enabling them to take necessary and timely actions. Women entrepreneurs demonstrate innovative and effective decision-making skills, which are essential for the profitability and productivity of their enterprises. They are known for their hard work and optimism, maintaining a positive outlook even when faced with challenges. Creativity and the ability to solve problems are also highlighted, along with strong interpersonal skills, which are essential for dealing with various stakeholders. Finally, leadership and team spirit are fundamental characteristics. Women entrepreneurs possess the ability to build and manage successful teams, demonstrating leadership by influencing and supporting others to work enthusiastically towards achieving common objectives (Acevedo-Duque et al., 2021).

Based on all the literature mentioned above and the important role of the female entrepreneur, it is noted that there is a significant interest in empowering female entrepreneurs around the globe.

3.2 Addressing the Motivations and Challenges for Female International Entrepreneurs

3.2.1 Motivations

International female entrepreneurs are often driven by financial (Chreim et al., 2018) or recognition-seeking motivations (Webster & Haandrikman, 2022). Literature on the reasons for female entrepreneurs to engage in self-employment on a global scale suggests that women's motivation is shaped based on different factors (Saridakis et al., 2014). These factors can be divided into 'push' or 'pull' factors. The 'Push' or negative factors are those associated with factors of needs (such as a marriage breakup migration). These factors can be linked to economic needs low-income prospects, or social needs such as frustration or little recognition as an employee or job dissatisfaction with low possibilities for advancement (Kobeissi, 2010). It is expected that female international entrepreneurs (if not linked to migration) will be more drawn to internationalisation.

The "pull" or positive factors are associated with factors of choice and the desire to pursue entrepreneurial activities (Orhan & Scott, 2001). Pull factors are more positive, personal (e.g., following their passion) or external (e.g., seeing a business opportunity), leading people and females to create businesses. In this case, the personal characteristics of the female are behind the creation of the business. These women are driven by their intrinsic goals and the desire for self-fulfilment (Poggesi et al., 2016), autonomy and emancipation (Harima et al., 2020; Rindova et al., 2009), financial benefit (Wilson et al., 2007), and to be a female role model by offering professional orientation (Noguera et al., 2013). Among the most essential motivations for women entrepreneurs is family motivation (Outsios & Farooqi, 2017). The goal of striking a balance between work and family (including childcare issues) motivates women entrepreneurs. As a result, they favour "self-employment," which allows for greater schedule flexibility (Saridakis et al., 2014). Moreover, other writers contended that female entrepreneurs might launch a company with the intention of "making a difference"(Still & Timms, 2000). They are driven to start a business by the social good that their company can provide to society and are more likely to do so with a community service orientation than with a profit-only mindset (Orhan & Scott, 2001).

Globally, according to the Global Entrepreneurship Monitor (2023) women reported starting a business more frequently than men did, citing job scarcity as a motivator and wanting to change the world (Fig. 3.1).

As illustrated from the figure below, the greatest reason given by most entrepreneurs for launching a business is a lack of employment; nearly two-thirds of men (67.2%) and almost three out of four women (72.9%) gave this explanation. Latin America and the Caribbean had the highest regional rates for women (82.2%).

3.2.2 Challenges

Women have struggled to break the "glass ceiling" and run their own businesses (Ughetto et al., 2020). The literature on female entrepreneurship has pointed to the challenges that women face in opening a business, making it grow, and bringing a more innovative environment and higher

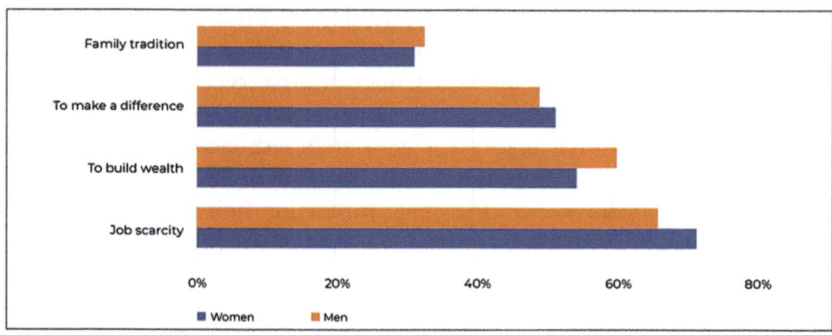

Fig. 3.1 Start-up motivations by gender. (*Source*: Global Entrepreneurship Monitor (GEM) 2022/2023 Women's Entrepreneurship Report: Challenging Bias and Stereotypes. https://www.gemconsortium.org/file/open?fileId=51352)

prospects of firm survival (Jennings & Brush, 2013; Wu et al., 2019). This literature focused on several female challenges to acquiring resources essential for spotting and pursuing a market opportunity (Kogut & Mejri, 2021). These challenges range from access to information and networks (Poggesi et al., 2016) and access to capital (Brush et al., 2009). For instance, female entrepreneurs struggle to receive funds from venture capital and bank loans (Marlow & McAdam, 2013). In addition to facing hurdles as entrepreneurs, women entrepreneurs also need to overcome other biases. For instance, female entrepreneurs still encounter constraints that often tend to be gender-specific (Jennings & Brush, 2013).

Depending on the type of push or pull factor that motivated them to become entrepreneurs, female international entrepreneurs will face different types of challenges. Female international entrepreneur may encounter higher obstacles in pursuing international entrepreneurial activities (Azmat, 2013) in comparison with their male counterparts.

It has been difficult for women to overcome the "glass ceiling" and launch their own companies (Ughetto et al., 2020). The literature on female entrepreneurship has highlighted the difficulties women encounter when starting and growing an international business (Jennings & Brush, 2013; Wu et al., 2019). This body of literature concentrated on the difficulties faced by women in obtaining the information needed to identify and seize global business opportunities (Kogut & Mejri, 2021). These difficulties include getting access to networks and information (Poggesi et al., 2016) as well as funding (Brush et al., 2009). For example, it can be difficult for women business owners to obtain bank loans and venture capital (Marlow & McAdam, 2013).

Female international entrepreneurs face gender-specific challenges and liabilities (Jennings & Brush, 2013), examples include the notion of "Motherhood," which represents the duties within the home and family environment (Brush et al., 2009), or the requirement to strike a balance between work and life (Agarwal & Lenka, 2015; Rey-Martí et al., 2015). This emphasises the significance of taking into account the family context in which they function (Aldrich & Cliff, 2003; Azmat & Fujimoto, 2016).

The liability of foreignness, a concept that is especially pertinent in international business literature and explains the disadvantages that foreigners face in comparison to locals, can have an impact on female international entrepreneurs (Zaheer, 1995). Its primary causes are "outsidership," which can keep foreigners out of local networks (Petersen & Pedersen, 2002), and information asymmetry, which results in foreigners knowing less and sometimes inaccurate information about the host nation (Eden & Miller, 2004; Johanson & Vahlne, 2009).

Additionally, female global entrepreneurs may reside in a foreign country where their religious and cultural backgrounds diverge, leaving them open to the "double stigma"—that is, the stigma associated with both migration and religion. (Moufakkir, 2020).

Lastly, the challenges associated with the businesses they launch—namely, the liabilities of smallness and newness—are faced by female international entrepreneurs (Barth & Zalkat, 2020) and smallness (Stinchcombe, 1965). Although the venture is described in the literature as being new, inexperienced, and resource-poor, the founder can also be held accountable for these characteristics. A lack of resources and experience can reduce the venture's potential for growth and raise the risk of failure. (Rey-Martí et al., 2015).

3.3 Transformative International Entrepreneurship

The internationalisation phenomenon has been studied for a long time, and a series of meanings and definitions have been attributed to it. In general, internationalisation is the growth of the firm outside of its national boundaries, and more precisely, it is regarded as growth and development in foreign markets. This phenomenon does not imply only the normal business activities of an enterprise abroad or, on the other hand, the influence that a firm has to maintain in its environment regarding foreign firm's business; it also involves a general flattening and mitigation of cultural or taste differences and, from an enterprise point of view, it means a growing standardisation of product characteristics and operational procedures which leads managers all over the world to run their business in an increasingly similar way (Levitt, 1983). Recently, in line with global transformation, the world has witnessed high-growth firms. These firms are known as 'gazelle' (Coad & Karlsson, 2022; Kotha et al., 2022), and are defined as 'enterprises up to 5 years old with average annualised growth greater than 20% per annum, over a three-year period (Eurostat-OECD, 2007, p. 63). Born Global/international new ventures are new phenomena that have emerged in the international entrepreneurship field.

Morrow (1988) introduced the term "International Entrepreneurship" (IE) to describe the evolving technological and cultural international environment that was opening previously untapped foreign markets to new ventures. From the beginning of the 1990s, studies on the subject have had impressive growth, ranging from contributions to the role of national culture (Wright & Ricks, 1994) to the practice of alliances and inter-firm cooperation (Steensma et al., 2000), with a dominant emphasis on the internationalisation of Small and Medium-Sized Enterprises (SMEs), on the entrepreneurial posture and background of top management teams, and on the role of venture financing.

Besides, the conduction of several additional studies (studies on small and medium-sized company internationalisation, entry modes (Zacharakis, 1997), corporate entrepreneurship (Birkinshaw, 1997), the publication of articles and the appearance of special issues and forums on international entrepreneurship in various journals, such as Entrepreneurship Theory and Practice in 1996 and Academy of Management Journal in 2000 have all helped to increase the interest in the arena, to broaden the field of international entrepreneurship from its early studies of new venture internationalisation theory, thus to move the field forward.

One of the first empirical studies in the area of international entrepreneurship was McDougall's (1989) work on new ventures' international sales. This study has provided important insights into the differences between these firms and those that did not start out on an international scale. The author defined international entrepreneurship "as the development of international new ventures or start-ups that, from their inception, engage in international business, thus viewing their operating domain as international from the initial stages of the firm's operation". (McDougall, 1989, p. 394)

In the early 1990s, McDougall and Oviatt further developed the study on the so-called "born-global firms" defined as "... a business organisation that, from inception, seeks to derive significant competitive advantage from the use of resources and sale of outputs in multiple countries." (McDougall et al., 1994, p. 49).

The definition of the boundaries of International Entrepreneurship has been discussed by many researchers: while some authors identify its domain in new ventures, others emphasise the construct of entrepreneurial behaviour, which can be observed in very different kinds of organisations (Zahra, 1993). for example, suggested that the study of international entrepreneurship should encompass both new firms and established companies, defining International Entrepreneurship as "the study of the nature and consequences of a firm's risk-taking behaviour as it ventures into international markets". International Entrepreneurship is observable at the organisational behaviour level and focuses on the relationship between businesses and the international environments in which they operate. In addition, other authors recognise that a firm's business environment plays an important role in influencing the expression of entrepreneurial activities (Zahra et al., 2005) and their returns. The importance of national cultures as "loci" for different expressions of International Entrepreneurship and the specific influence of the business environment emphasise the need for comparative studies as one of the areas of interest in International Entrepreneurship.

In 2000, Oviatt and McDougall introduced a broader definition of international entrepreneurship, including the study of established companies and the recognition of comparative (cross-national) analysis. They defined this field as "a combination of innovative, proactive, and risk-seeking behaviour that crosses or is compared across national borders and is intended to create value in business organisations."(McDougall & Oviatt, 2000, p. 903). This definition considers entrepreneurship as a phenomenon at the organisational level that focuses on innovation, risk-taking and proactive behaviour. It also focuses on the entrepreneurial behaviour of these firms rather than studying only the characteristics and intentions of the individual entrepreneurs. The key dimensions of entrepreneurship—innovativeness, proactiveness and risk propensity—can be found and developed at the organisational level. Innovativeness reflects a tendency to support new ideas, experimentation and new processes, while proactiveness refers to the capacity to anticipate and act on future needs and desires. Lastly, risk-taking conduct indicates the will to commit resources and be fully aware that the potential for failure may be high.

Including established companies in the study permits us to make the assumption that well-established companies can also be innovative and risk-taking, correcting an oversight in the entrepreneurship field. Many highly regarded, well-established companies work hard to foster innovation, support venturing, and encourage risk-taking.

The process supporting international entrepreneurial orientation is described by Shane and Venkataraman (2000) as a process of discovery, and this seems to correspond to what Weick (1995) describes as enactment. Consequently, the definitions of IE and the object of analysis tend to move from specific subjects (given typologies of firms, with their industries and markets, and their international behaviour) to organisational attributes, grounded on entrepreneurship literature, and to firm resources and capabilities. The Oviatt and McDougall (2005) definition makes it difficult to recognise international entrepreneurship in terms of easily observable factors (age, size, industry) and imposes a deeper understanding of firm resources, processes and behaviour (Oviatt & McDougall, 2005).

The evolution in the definitions of IE proposed by different authors suggests that an expression of international entrepreneurship is not the entry per se in a foreign market, but it is a combination of attitudes at the individual and organisational level (proactiveness, innovativeness, risk-seeking) and of actions over time, along an evolutionary and potentially discontinuous process.

3.3.1 Born Global and International New Ventures

BGs are known to be entrepreneurial and international in their business dealings. There are many international entrepreneurial SME firms that internationalise steadily but at a relatively slow pace. However, academic researchers have observed accelerated internationalisation

The growing importance of this new phenomenon seems to challenge most of the already established theories on internationalisation and, in particular, process stages theories of the Uppsala School model. This theory that considers internationalisation as a process of gradual commitment, including a progressive number of stages in a relatively long period of time, has been challenged. Some advocates of accelerated international entrepreneurship have, in fact, identified an increasing number of firms that were rapidly present abroad after their birth instead of following the traditional path that presupposes domestic expansion before foreign export activities in psychically and geographically close markets. The existence of this typology of firms has been verified by empirical studies in both low- and high-tech industries, and the geographical localisation has also been heterogeneous.

Moreover, a significant part of the International New Venture and Born-Global literature, especially in the first years of establishment, has been assumed to apply largely to high-tech businesses since the effects of globalisation were easily detected in these sectors. Nonetheless, some researchers have shown that it is not limited to such sectors. Indeed, they have shown that the phenomenon also occurs in sectors such as the footwear industries. "the "high-tech bias" may lead research to indicate the industry/product as a qualifying feature of born-global firms, while it is only one of their possible attributes'.

An important proof of the existence of other international entrepreneurial entities is given by some companies, especially small-medium firms that show typical entrepreneurial characteristics, but they are neither born-globals because they do not develop international activities from their foundation nor subsidiaries because they are not linked to any Multinational enterprise. In 2001, Jim Bell and his colleagues defined a group of firms that might be a subject of International Entrepreneurship: the "Born-Again Global" (BAG) firms: "These are firms that have been well established in their domestic markets, with apparently no great motivation to internationalise, but which have suddenly embraced rapid and dedicated internationalisation". (Bell et al., 2001). These firms seem not to have a precise collocation within International Entrepreneurial models, but nevertheless, they demonstrate proactive behaviour, own knowledge-based resources and show a receptive attitude to international opportunities, which are all common characteristics of the two other typologies of international entrepreneurial firms.

3.3.2 Rising and Emergence of Unicorn Start-up

Businesses can grow in a multitude of ways, and these growth patterns are not random; they can vary significantly over time and be attributed to a multitude of factors.

The term "unicorn start-ups" refers to privately held, fast-growing start-up businesses valued at one billion dollars or more. It was initially used in 2013 by Cowboy Ventures founder Aileen Lee (De Massis et al., 2016). With a total cumulative worth of more than $3800 billion, there are already 1200 unicorns in the world (CBInsights, 2023). According to (UNCTAD, 2021), innovative start-ups assume the lead, expand, and pose a threat to established companies. These incredibly innovative and progressive venture forms have become a "hot topic" in the practitioner literature, usually limited to venture capital talks (Kenney & Zysman, 2019) or media reports.

"A Unicorn start-up is a super-gazelle with a concrete and excessively ambitious growth target," according to (Kuckertz et al., 2023, p. 2). The last ten years have seen a number of research studies on the formation or success of unicorn start-ups, drawn by the successful journeys of unicorns (De Massis et al., 2016; Dellermann et al., 2021; Jinzhi & Carrick, 2019). Kabbara and Hagen (2023) looked into a number of factors that affect the life cycle and the high growth of Unicorn in the long term. Unicorns refute the notion that start-up challenges are inherently associated with the risk of novelty (Cristofaro et al., 2023). The earlier stages of emergence and growth have received the majority of attention in current work, but the longer-term perspective has been disregarded. They are described as "mythical creatures" by other academics (Kuckertz et al., 2023). Because of this, the idea of unicorn start-ups as a subset of high-growth firms (HGFs) is currently the subject of intense debate and a dispersed research field (Aldrich & Ruef, 2020), which heightens interest in this emerging phenomenon. The Unicorn Club has members from 47 different countries worldwide, according to the CB Insights Unicorn list, which is widely regarded as the definitive list of Unicorns (Gornall & Strebulaev, 2020). Since October 2022, it has grown from 1191 to 1205 Unicorns, a 1.2% increase. According to CB Insights (2023), there were over 1200 unicorns in the world as of January 2023, and their combined market value exceeded $3800 billion. The United States accounted for 53,9% of these unicorns, followed by China (14,3%), India (5,7%), and the United Kingdom (4,2%). Approximately one in five unicorns belong to the fintech industry, which is the largest category (21%).

3.4 Drivers of Transformative Firms' Growth

3.4.1 Born Global Firms 'Growth

Development drivers of born global firms in the last decade are far from being completely explored; it vary from "environmental" factors, such as world market globalisation, and industry, to business-specific factors, networks and the entrepreneur.

The theory of Born-Globals has its origin in Entrepreneurship theory, where the internationalisation process of born-global firms is considered to be initiated by the entrepreneur with an innovative, proactive and risk-taking approach (McDougall & Oviatt, 2000). This process can also be the result of mental models possessed by the Top Management Team, especially in corporate ventures. Managers in Born-Globals have, to a great extent, the experience of international settings, international contacts and a more positive attitude toward internationalisation, which influences the firm's possibilities of success in the international market. Etemad and Lee (2003) have shown the importance of networks as drivers of small-firm internationalisation and as an important factor during foreign market selection, selection of mode of entry, product development and market diversification activities. The social and inter-organisational networks, as well as dyadic alliances, are gatekeepers to opportunities for exploration and exploitation (Kabbara, 2009). Their role is fundamental for firms, which are characterised either by the joint effect of the liability of newness and foreignness or, in general, by risk-taking and resource-consuming accelerated internationalisation processes (Zucchella & Kabbara, 2013). Moreover, the firm's local environment and its geographical location influence the internationalisation process of Born-Globals. Studies conducted in Italy (Zucchella & Kabbara, 2011), Portugal and New Zealand show that growing interest is increased in local clusters, where firms within a specific industry are situated in a geographic region or an industrial district.

3.4.2 Unicorn Start-up Growth

The bulk of research on high-growth firms has clarified the relationship between founding teams and firm-specific characteristics and organisational growth in general and high growth in particular (Moreno & Casillas, 2007; Satterthwaite & Hamilton, 2017).

At different levels of analysis, numerous studies in the literature on international entrepreneurship have tried to pinpoint the factors that contribute to the expansion of foreign new ventures. As examples, some academics have emphasised the importance of these drivers as catalysts for born global growth and international expansion at the firm level, entrepreneur level (Kabbara, 2016), and macro-level (Jafari-Sadeghi et al., 2019).

The success and expansion of new technology-based businesses have been linked to the founder's human capital, according to earlier research. According to the authors, more successful high-tech start-up growth is established by founders with higher education levels and more experience, particularly in the same industry as the new firm (i.e., industry-specific human capital), which is obtained either through a managerial position in another firm or through previous episodes of self-employment. Additionally, studies on entrepreneurial finance indicate that founders of new technology companies with higher human capital will be able to draw in more venture capital, which will lead to higher growth.

Numerous authors highlight the significance of digital business models and digitalisation as major forces behind company expansion. For example, in order to improve business model innovation, create new revenue streams, and seize opportunities for value creation, companies need to adopt digital technologies that are accessible and affordable for small businesses Digitalisation may have a number of benefits for SMEs, such as increased output, better decision-making and product quality and process efficiency, increased flexibility, shorter time to market, creation of new business models, a new role for the customer, and environmental sustainability (Chen & Perez, 2018).

Moreover, inter-organisational firm networks—which are defined as external relationships and partnerships—are a source for the expansion and competitiveness of entrepreneurial firms. The literature on international and high-growth entrepreneurship holds that a company's network plays a critical role in its valuation. Network importance is especially important for businesses that use online business models.

Furthermore, the literature has emphasised the role that industries play in the expansion of businesses. For example, when a venture seeks venture capital financing in its early stages of development, the industry's attractiveness, among other factors (like the founder's qualifications and external relationships), has a significant and positive impact on venture capitalists' valuation, which in turn affects the venture's high-growth.

Technological waves create substantial advancements and widespread acceptance of new technologies, resulting in transformative changes in various industries and society as a whole. The widespread use of the mobile internet since the early 2000s has not only changed the way people communicate and interact but has also opened the door for a huge number of creative and innovative start-ups. The rise of unicorn start-ups has been facilitated by a rapidly expanding consumer market, low entry barriers in terms of cost, and significant availability of private capital, including venture capital (VC) and equity. The number of unicorns has increased in sectors driven by digitalisation. In the following, the aforementioned factors will be further discussed as they have played a crucial role in the development of unicorn start-ups. Starting a business was highly challenging a few decades ago, but today, new businesses are founded all over the world every day. The accessibility and convenience of the mobile internet have created countless opportunities for entrepreneurs to connect with a market of increasingly tech-savvy customers. Most people around the world own a smartphone and are familiar with apps, which has helped businesses grow on a global scale. Additionally, the relatively low barriers to entry into the mobile market have made it easier than ever for ambitious entrepreneurs to pursue their ideas and start their own businesses.

Kenney and Zysman (2019) argue that the cost of starting a business has decreased significantly, mostly due to the falling cost of computing and the rise of cloud-based operations. The availability of software tools and services from providers like Amazon Web Services and Microsoft Azure has allowed start-ups to rent server capacity rather than invest money in their own IT infrastructure. Furthermore, open-source software, such as GitHub, helps companies reduce costs and time to market by eliminating the need to code from scratch.

Investors are convinced that start-ups have the potential to generate significant financial returns. This is due to disruptive advances in information and communication technology (ICT), such as big data, smartphones, machine learning and the Internet of Things. In combination with start-ups' innovative business models, investors are recognising their potential to revolutionise established economic sectors (Kenney & Zysman, 2019. The increased growth and success potential of start-ups has been further boosted by the accessibility of capital and the variety of funding options. Compared to previous decades, venture capital investors now manage higher amounts of money and have larger funds in start-ups.

(Kenney & Zysman, 2019) describes that they are highly willing to support the financial needs of early-stage start-ups that are not publicly traded on the stock exchange markets. Moreover, there are a large number of players in the venture funding landscape, such as angel investors, mainstream venture capitalists, small venture capitalists, private equity (PE) and hedge funds. This diversity of funding options means that start-ups are less dependent on a single investor.

Another factor that has accelerated the emergence of some unicorns was the Covid-19 pandemic mentioned above. As a result of the pandemic, several start-ups demonstrated their willingness to adapt and innovate their business models. They successfully overcame the obstacles of the crisis by expanding their partner networks, implementing appropriate payment services, and using new digital communication platforms. As a result, the global pandemic has accelerated the digital transformation across several industries. Unicorns have managed to significantly increase their value in the sectors of fintech, internet, software, e-commerce, and AI services. Fintech companies are at the forefront of addressing the increasing need for digital transactions. Finally, technology-based start-ups need to be highly interested in adapting to uncertain situations as they open possibilities in different markets.

3.5 CASE STUDY OF A GLOBAL FEMALE ENTREPRENEUR IN THE COSMETIC INDUSTRY

Hudabeauty Brand was selected as a case study subject because she is an American global entrepreneur who is working in the cosmetic industry. The most well-known American makeup artist, Huda Kattan, who later became a global businesswoman of a company with over 3000 locations across 45 countries, Huda Beauty is a billion-dollar company that specialises in makeup, skincare, and fragrances.

This case was chosen as an appropriate example to examine how a global female entrepreneur faced challenges and how she managed to become global by leveraging as well on social media.

HUDA BEAUTY
Building a Community

Launched by award-winning beauty blogger Huda Kattan in 2013, Huda Beauty is one of the world's fastest-growing beauty brands. Beginning as a blog in 2010, Huda Beauty has fast become the number 1 Beauty Instagram account in the world with over 26 million followers and counting! A lifelong passion for beauty led Huda to enrol at a prestigious makeup training school in Los Angeles, cultivating a roster of clientele, including A-list celebrities and members of a royal family. Soon after, Huda set up her beauty blog, HUDABEAUTY.COM, and later launched a YouTube channel and an Instagram account using the same name.

"I've always been extremely passionate and the type of person who loves sharing information! When I first started my career in beauty, I worked as a makeup artist, which I absolutely loved, but I still felt like something was missing. I wanted to help others by sharing the tricks I had learned and acknowledge all of the incredibly talented makeup artists, photographers and models in the industry. I knew that beauty sometimes felt a bit unattainable and cold and I really wanted to change that. Ultimately, Hudabeauty.com became a place for people to feel beautiful and comfortable and to share their own inspiration and thoughts around beauty."

Innovation and Inspiration

2013 was the turning point for Huda as she and her sisters Mona and Alya worked together to create a collection of false eyelashes under the Huda Beauty brand name, which would later launch at Sephora in Dubai Mall. Huda's experience in the beauty industry has allowed her to expand the range to include liquid lipsticks, lip contour pencils, textured eyeshadow palettes and complexion products—all of which have been instant best-sellers across the globe.

"Working as a makeup artist, I wasn't satisfied with the style and quality of lashes that were available at the time, so I often ended up stacking and customising the lashes myself to suit the client's eye shape. After receiving several messages from people wanting to buy

(continued)

> (continued)
> the lashes I had customised, my sister Mona suggested I start my own line. My older sister Alya was the initial investor; she invested $6,500 for our first batch of products. I have been a blogger, I have created social content, I have worked as a makeup artist, I have worked with manufacturers to create products in the lab, and I am the face of a brand. My experience in the industry has allowed me to really appreciate and understand the industry and look at it from different angles. We have a very engaged community that is always telling us what they want to see, so we take a lot of inspiration from the comments we see on social media and only create products that there is a demand for."
>
> Source: Hudabeauty.com website

According to a recent interview with Huda published on Vogue by Manual Arnaut (26 January 2023), Kattan, ten years ago, worked from her kitchen counter to create a set of fake eyelashes using a US $6 000 loan from her sister following her dismissal from a position as a financial recruiter. The new product was introduced only at Sephora, where it was immediately successful because the blogger had a devoted following from years of blogging. "When she introduced her brand in Dubai, nobody had any idea what would happen to it; it was completely risky." She then wonders if managing a company that is still expanding gets easier or harder over time in light of the widespread praise. The first collaboration was with Sephora, who agreed to sell her first new product, 'faux lashes. 'She feels she has more responsibilities and a larger machine to run even though she is more experienced in the field. Although things in the world are constantly changing, she feels that she truly knows what she is doing and that she can trust herself. However, it happened that She occasionally hired specialists to advise her on what would be best for her company, but eventually, she came to the conclusion that she needed to stop paying attention to their advice. Nobody will perform what she does with the same passion as she does because it comes from the bottom of her heart. Concerns about the brand's ethical and sustainable practices also damage the brand's reputation. As a result, the company begins to lose market share, which forces Huda to make some different choices.

Self-assured and determined In late 2024, Huda made the decision to take back her position as CEO of Hudabeauty in an effort to win back customer trust.

The brand is presently going through a comprehensive rebranding, which includes brand identity, packaging, and logo

Her sisters and family are involved in the business with her. When Kattan shared a joyful photo of herself online in a red lace bodysuit, she became the target of an online attack in the world of social media and digital platforms. The look was too provocative, as some of her over 50 million followers quickly pointed out. Because of her high emotional intelligence, she was able to turn the unpleasant situation into a teaching moment by compiling the cruellest comments into a video. She clarified that she makes an effort to wear whatever she wants. She continued by saying that she tries to avoid dressing in a way that is too provocative because of her religious obligations. Keeping an optimistic outlook, Kattan is not afraid to acknowledge that, thanks in part to her growing prominence, wealth, and responsibility, she has changed as a woman. She needed to grow, but she continued to be modest.

From this example, it is clear that successful global women entrepreneurs must overcome a number of obstacles and setbacks. Huda always had a strong sense of self-confidence and a passion for entrepreneurship. When Huda cut off contact with her customers, her business began to suffer. She became anxious about re-establishing positive connections and a network with her customers.

Despite facing a lot of criticism regarding her brand's ethical practices, she managed to remain resilient and flexible, implementing sustainable practices and making an effort to communicate publicly with her customers. These choices had a positive effect on her company's survival and growth.

This case demonstrates that the motivation behind global entrepreneurship is the need to follow a passion for makeup; she started to make makeup for her family and friends, and then made such tutorial makeup online. She felt there was a demand from the consumer. She has limited access to finance. She took a loan from her sister, stressing the importance of family as a social capital. She didn't have a specific place; she started from her kitchen, and she decided to take a risk and launch her new product, believing in herself and that she could make it. Encouraged and inspired by her family, Huda made the decision to launch a new product. She worked with one of the biggest cosmetic retailers, Sephora. She was able to reach a broad audience of customers by doing this and promoting her new product. This emphasises how she partnered with major stakeholders and used her network to cope with her liability of newness, highlighting the importance of partnerships in the companies' internationalisation process. A key element in her success was her passion for makeup artists and her fervent desire to start her own business. It's interesting to observe that, in this instance, networking and passion mitigate the disadvantages of newness and gender.

The female global entrepreneur's family—mainly her sisters—turned out to be crucial in helping her overcome her financial challenges, proving that, in this case, the family acts as the central support system for the (international) entrepreneurial process and enables the woman to progressively become acknowledged as a successful female entrepreneur.

REFERENCES

Acevedo-Duque, Á., Gonzalez-Diaz, R., Vargas, E. C., Paz-Marcano, A., Muller-Pérez, S., Salazar-Sepúlveda, G., et al. (2021). Resilience, leadership and female entrepreneurship within the context of smes: Evidence from latin america. *Sustainability, 13*(15), 8129.

Agarwal, S., & Lenka, U. (2015). Study on work-life balance of women entrepreneurs–review and research agenda. *Industrial and Commercial Training*.

Aldrich, H. E., & Cliff, J. E. (2003). The pervasive effects of family on entrepreneurship: Toward a family embeddedness perspective. *Journal of Business Venturing, 18*(5), 573–596.

Aldrich, H. E., & Ruef, M. (2020). Scholars should study everyday entrepreneurs, not gazelles. *Entrepreneur & Innovation Exchange*.

Arregle, J. L., Batjargal, B., Hitt, M. A., Webb, J. W., Miller, T., & Tsui, A. S. (2015). Family ties in entrepreneurs' social networks and new venture growth. *Entrepreneurship Theory and Practice, 39*(2), 313–344.

Ascher, J. (2012). Female entrepreneurship—an appropriate response to gender discrimination. *Journal of Entrepreneurship, Management and Innovation, 8*(4), 97–114.

Azmat, F. (2013). Opportunities or obstacles? Understanding the challenges faced by migrant women entrepreneurs. *International Journal of Gender and Entrepreneurship, 5*(2), 198–215.

Azmat, F., & Fujimoto, Y. (2016). Family embeddedness and entrepreneurship experience: A study of Indian migrant women entrepreneurs in Australia. *Entrepreneurship & Regional Development, 28*(9–10), 630–656.

Barth, H., & Zalkat, G. (2020). Immigrant entrepreneurship in Sweden: The liability of newness. *Sustainability, 12*(16), 6478.

Bell, J., McNaughton, R., & Young, S. (2001). 'Born-again global' firms: An extension to the 'born global' phenomenon. *Journal of International Management, 7*(3), 173–189.

Birkinshaw, J. (1997). Entrepreneurship in multinational corporations: The characteristics of subsidiary initiatives. *Strategic Management Journal, 18*, 207–229.

Bruni, A., Gherardi, S., & Poggio, B. (2004). Entrepreneur-mentality, Gender and the Study of Women Entrepreneurs. *Journal of Organizational Change Management 17*(3 High Growth Women's Entrepreneurship), 256–268.

Brush, C., Edelman, L. F., Manolova, T., & Welter, F. (2019). A gendered look at entrepreneurship ecosystems. *Small Business Economics, 53*(2), 393–408.

Brush, C. G., De Bruin, A., & Welter, F. (2009). A gender-aware framework for women's entrepreneurship. *International Journal of Gender and Entrepreneurship.*

CBInsights. (2023). The complete list of Unicorns companies.

Chen, Y., & Perez, Y. (2018). Business model design: Lessons learned from Tesla Motors. In *Towards a sustainable economy* (pp. 53–69). Springer.

Chreim, S., Spence, M., Crick, D., & Liao, X. L. (2018). Review of female immigrant entrepreneurship research: Past findings, gaps and ways forward. *European Management Journal, 36*(2), 210–222.

Chrysostome, E., & Lin, X. (2010). Immigrant entrepreneurship: Scrutinizing a promising type of business venture. *Thunderbird International Business Review, 52*(2), 77–82.

Coad, A., & Karlsson, J. (2022). A field guide for gazelle hunters: Small, old firms are unlikely to become high-growth firms. *Journal of Business Venturing Insights, 17*, e00286.

Cristofaro, M., Giannetti, F., & Abatecola, G. (2023). The initial survival of the Unicorns: A behavioral perspective of Snapchat. *Journal of Management History.*

Crittenden, V. L., Crittenden, W. F., & Ajjan, H. (2019). Empowering women micro-entrepreneurs in emerging economies: The role of information communications technology. *Journal of Business Research, 98*, 191–203.

De Massis, A., Frattini, F., & Quillico, F. (2016). What big companies can learn from the success of the unicorns. *Harvard Business Review*, 1–5.

Dean, H., Larsen, G., Ford, J., & Akram, M. (2019). Female entrepreneurship and the metanarrative of economic growth: A critical review of underlying assumptions. *International Journal of Management Reviews, 21*(1), 24–49.

Dellermann, D., Lipusch, N., Ebel, P., Popp, K. M., & Leimeister, J. M. (2021). Finding the unicorn: Predicting early stage startup success through a hybrid intelligence method. *arXiv preprint arXiv:2105.03360*.

Díaz-García, M. C., & Jiménez-Moreno, J. (2010). Entrepreneurial intention: The role of gender. *International Entrepreneurship and Management Journal, 6*(3), 261–283.

Discua Cruz, A., Howorth, C., & Hamilton, E. (2013). Intrafamily entrepreneurship: The formation and membership of family entrepreneurial teams. *Entrepreneurship Theory and Practice, 37*(1), 17–46.

Eden, L., & Miller, S. R. (2004). Distance matters: Liability of foreignness, institutional distance and ownership strategy. In *Theories of the multinational enterprise: Diversity, complexity and relevance* (Vol. 16, pp. 187–221). Emerald Group Publishing Limited.

Etemad, H., & Lee, Y. (2003). The knowledge network of international entrepreneurship: Theory and evidence. *Small Business Economics, 20*(1), 5–23.

Eurostat-OECD. (2007). On business demography statistics.

Ezzedeen, S. R., & Zikic, J. (2017). Finding balance amid boundarylessness: An interpretive study of entrepreneurial work-life balance and boundary management. *Journal of Family Issues, 38*(11), 1546–1576.

GEM (Global Entrepreneurship Monitor) (2022/2023). *Adapting to a new normal*. Available at: https://gemconsortium.org/report/20222023-global-entrepreneurship-monitor-global-report-adapting-to-a-newnormal-2/ (accessed 16 October 2024).

Gornall, W., & Strebulaev, I. A. (2020). Squaring venture capital valuations with reality. *Journal of Financial Economics, 135*(1), 120–143.

Harima, A., Harima, J., & Freiling, J. (2020). The injection of resources by transnational entrepreneurs: Towards a model of the early evolution of an entrepreneurial ecosystem. *Entrepreneurship & Regional Development, 33*(1–2), 80–107.

Hechavarria, D. M., Terjesen, S. A., Ingram, A. E., Renko, M., Justo, R., & Elam, A. (2017). Taking care of business: The impact of culture and gender on entrepreneurs' blended value creation goals. *Small Business Economics, 48*(1), 225–257.

Jafari-Sadeghi, V., Garcia-Perez, A., Candelo, E., & Couturier, J. (2021). Exploring the impact of digital transformation on technology entrepreneurship and technological market expansion: The role of technology readiness, exploration and exploitation. *Journal of Business Research, 124*, 100–111.

Jafari-Sadeghi, V., Kimiagari, S., & Biancone, P. P. (2019). Level of education and knowledge, foresight competency and international entrepreneurship: A study of human capital determinants in the European countries. *European Business Review*.

Jakhar, R., & Krishna, C. (2020). Women entrepreneurship: opportunities and challenges (a literature review). *Anwesh, 5*(2), p. 38.

Jennings, J. E., & Brush, C. G. (2013). Research on women entrepreneurs: Challenges to (and from) the broader entrepreneurship literature? *Academy of Management Annals, 7*(1), 663–715.

Jinzhi, Z., & Carrick, J. (2019). The rise of the Chinese unicorn: An exploratory study of unicorn companies in China. *Emerging Markets Finance and Trade, 55*(15), 3371–3385.

Johanson, J., & Vahlne, J. E. (2009). The Uppsala internationalization process model revisited: From liability of foreignness to liability of outsidership. *Journal of International Business Studies, 40*(9), 1411–1431.

Kabbara, D. (2009). The evolutionary network process of international entrepreneurial firms. *International Journal of Globalisation and Small Business, 3*(3), 346–370.

Kabbara, D. (2016). The influence of the entrepreneur and the accelerator in the internationalization process of web-based firms. In *The changing global economy and its impact on international entrepreneurship*. Edward Elgar Publishing.

Kabbara, D., & Hagen, B. (2023). A life cycle view on unicorn start-ups: Drivers of long-term high-growth. *Journal of Small Business and Enterprise Development, 30*(6), 1210–1240.

Kabbara, D., & Zucchella, A. (2013). Social networks and inter-organizationalties of knowledge-intensive firms (KIFs). In *Current issues in international entrepreneurship*. Edward Elgar Publishing.

Kenney, M., & Zysman, J. (2019). Unicorns, Cheshire cats, and the new dilemmas of entrepreneurial finance. *Venture Capital, 21*(1), 35–50.

Kobeissi, N. (2010). Gender factors and female entrepreneurship: International evidence and policy implications. *Journal of International Entrepreneurship, 8*(1), 1–35.

Kogut, C. S., & Mejri, K. (2021). Female entrepreneurship in emerging markets: Challenges of running a business in turbulent contexts and times. *International Journal of Gender and Entrepreneurship*.

Kotha, S., Shin, S. J., & Fisher, G. (2022). Time to unicorn status: An exploratory examination of new ventures with extreme valuations. *Strategic Entrepreneurship Journal, 16*(3), 460–490.

Kuckertz, A., Scheu, M., & Davidsson, P. (2023). Chasing mythical creatures–A (not-so-sympathetic) critique of entrepreneurship's obsession with unicorn startups. *Journal of Business Venturing Insights, 19*, e00365.

Levitt, T. (1983). The globalization of markets. *Harvard Business Review*, May–June, 92–102.

Manello, A., Cisi, M., Devicienti, F., & Vannoni, D. (2020). Networking: A business for women. *Small Business Economics, 55*(2), 329–348.

March, J. G. (1991). Exploration and exploitation in organizational learning. *Organization Science, 2*(1), 71–87.

Marlow, S., & McAdam, M. (2013). Gender and entrepreneurship: Advancing debate and challenging myths; exploring the mystery of the under-performing female entrepreneur. *International Journal of Entrepreneurial Behavior & Research*.

McAdam, M., Harrison, R. T., & Leitch, C. M. (2019). Stories from the field: Women's networking as gender capital in entrepreneurial ecosystems. *Small Business Economics*, 53(2), 459–474.

McDougall, P. P. (1989). International versus domestic entrepreneurship: New venture strategic behavior and industry structure. *Journal of Business Venturing*, 4(6), 387–400.

McDougall, P. P., & Oviatt, B. M. (2000). International entrepreneurship: The intersection of two research paths. *Academy of Management Journal*, 43(5), 902–906.

McDougall, P. P., Shane, S., & Oviatt, B. M. (1994). Explaining the formation of international new ventures: The limits of theories from international business research. *Journal of Business Venturing*, 9(6), 469–487.

Morrow, J. F. (1988). International entrepreneurship: A new growth opportunity. *New Management*, 5(3), 59–60.

Moreno, A. M., & Casillas, J. C. (2007). High-growth SMEs versus non-high-growth SMEs: A discriminant analysis. *Entrepreneurship and Regional Development*, 19(1), 69–88.

Moufakkir, O. (2020). Experience of Arab/Muslim women visiting relatives in the West and the management of stigma by association. *Tourism Management*, 78, 104073.

Munkejord, M. C. (2017). Local and transnational networking among female immigrant entrepreneurs in peripheral rural contexts: Perspectives on Russians in Finnmark, Norway. *European Urban and Regional Studies*, 24(1), 7–20.

Mustafa, M., & Chen, S. (2010). The strength of family networks in transnational immigrant entrepreneurship. *Thunderbird International Business Review*, 52(2), 97–106.

Noguera, M., Alvarez, C., & Urbano, D. (2013). Socio-cultural factors and female entrepreneurship. *International Entrepreneurship and Management Journal*, 9(2), 183–197.

Onyusheva, I., & Meyer, N. (2020). The features of female entrepreneurship development in Kazakhstan: an analytical survey. *Polish Journal of Management Studies*, 21(1), 265–282.

Orhan, M., & Scott, D. (2001). Why women enter into entrepreneurship: An explanatory model. *Women in Management Review*.

Outsios, G., & Farooqi, S. A. (2017). Gender in sustainable entrepreneurship: Evidence from the UK. *Gender in Management: An International Journal*.

Oviatt, B. M., & McDougall, P. P. (2005). Defining international entrepreneurship and modeling the speed of internationalization. *Entrepreneurship Theory and Practice, 29*(5), 537–553.

Petersen, B., & Pedersen, T. (2002). Coping with liability of foreignness: Different learning engagements of entrant firms. *Journal of International Management, 8*(3), 339–350.

Poggesi, S., Mari, M., & De Vita, L. (2016). What's new in female entrepreneurship research? Answers from the literature. *International Entrepreneurship and Management Journal, 12*(3), 735–764.

Pruthi, S., Basu, A., & Wright, M. (2018). Ethnic ties, motivations, and home country entry strategy of transnational entrepreneurs. *Journal of International Entrepreneurship, 16*(2), 210–243.

Rehman, S., & Roomi, M. A. (2012). Gender and work-life balance: A phenomenological study of women entrepreneurs in Pakistan. *Journal of Small Business and Enterprise Development.*

Rey-Martí, A., Porcar, A. T., & Mas-Tur, A. (2015). Linking female entrepreneurs' motivation to business survival. *Journal of Business Research, 68*(4), 810–814.

Ribes-Giner, G., Moya-Clemente, I., Cervelló-Royo, R., & Perello-Marin, M. R. (2018). Domestic economic and social conditions empowering female entrepreneurship. *Journal of Business Research, 89,* 182–189.

Rindova, V., Barry, D., & Ketchen, D. J. (2009). Entrepreneuring as emancipation. *Academy of Management Review, 34*(3), 477–491.

Saridakis, G., Marlow, S., & Storey, D. J. (2014). Do different factors explain male and female self-employment rates? *Journal of Business Venturing, 29*(3), 345–362.

Satterthwaite, S., & Hamilton, R. (2017). High-growth firms in New Zealand: Superstars or shooting stars? *International Small Business Journal, 35*(3), 244–261.

Shane, S., & Venkataraman, S. (2000). The promise of entrepreneurship as a field of research. *Academy of Management Review, 25*(1), 217–226.

Steensma, K., Marino, L., Weaver, M., & Dickson, P. (2000). The influence of national culture in the formation of technology alliances by entrepreneurial firms. *Academy of Management Journal, 43,* 951–73.

Still, L. V., & Timms, W. (2000). Women's business: The flexible alternative workstyle for women. *Women in Management Review.*

Stinchcombe, A. L. (1965). Organizations and social structure. *Handbook of Organizations, 44*(2), 142–193.

Sussan, F., & Acs, Z. J. (2017). The digital entrepreneurial ecosystem. *Small Business Economics, 49*(1), 55–73.

Ughetto, E., Rossi, M., Audretsch, D., & Lehmann, E. E. (2020). Female entrepreneurship in the digital era. *Small Business Economics, 55*(2), 305–312.

UNCTAD. (2021). The creative economy programme. Retrieved December 16, 2021, from https://unctad.org/topic/trade-analysis/creative-economy-programme

Webster, N. A., & Haandrikman, K. (2022). Exploring the role of privilege in migrant women's self-employment. *Entrepreneurship Theory and Practice, 46*(6), 1534–1568.

Wilson, F., Kickul, J., & Marlino, D. (2007). Gender, entrepreneurial self–efficacy, and entrepreneurial career intentions: Implications for entrepreneurship education. *Entrepreneurship Theory and Practice, 31*(3), 387–406.

Wright, R.W., and Ricks, D.A. (1994). "Trends in international business research: Twenty-five years later". *Journal of International Business Studies, 25*(4) 687–701.

Wu, J., Li, Y. K., & Zhang, D. R. (2019). Identifying women's entrepreneurial barriers and empowering female entrepreneurship worldwide: A fuzzy-set QCA approach. *International Entrepreneurship and Management Journal, 15*(3), 905–928.

Zacharakis, A. L. (1997). Entrepreneurial entry into foreign markets: A transaction cost perspective. *Entrepreneurship Theory and Practice, 21*, 23–39.

Zaheer, S. (1995). Overcoming the liability of foreignness. *Academy of Management Journal, 38*(2), 341–363.

Zahra, S. A. (1993). A conceptual model of entrepreneurship as firm behavior: A critique and extension. *Entrepreneurship Theory and Practice, 17*(4), 5–21.

Zahra, S. A., Korri, J. S., & Yu, J. (2005). Cognition and international entrepreneurship: Implications for research on international opportunity recognition and exploitation. *International Business Review, 14*(2), 129–146.

Zucchella, A. (2021). International entrepreneurship and the internationalization phenomenon: Taking stock, looking ahead. *International Business Review, 30*(2), 101800.

Zucchella, A., & Kabbara, D. (2011). Collaborative entrepreneurship and internationalization in life sciences: Global growth through collaboration in Italian Biotech Firms. In *International entrepreneurship in the life sciences.* Edward Elgar Publishing.

Zucchella, A., & Kabbara, D. (2013). The role of partnerships in the internationalisation process of small knowledge intensive firms (SKIFs). *Management International/International Management/Gestión Internacional, 18*(1), 104–116.

CHAPTER 4

Digital Entrepreneurship: Empowering Female Entrepreneurs

Abstract As the landscape of global challenges such as poverty, inequality, and climate change becomes increasingly complex, integrating digital technologies into the entrepreneurial process becomes paramount. In the digital age, female entrepreneurship is a transformative force that gives women previously unheard-of chances to launch, run, and expand their businesses. Gender barriers have been broken down by the emergence of digital platforms and technologies, which have democratised access to markets, networks, and resources. Digital transformation enables female entrepreneurs to leverage technological advancements to address these challenges effectively, making it a key component of international entrepreneurship. This holistic approach not only drives economic growth but also enhances the quality of life of the female and fosters global cooperation. This chapter will address the significant role of technology in the entrepreneurial context and in empowering female digital entrepreneurship. The chapter will also cover how technology affects female entrepreneurs personally and professionally and highlight the trade-off of technology on female digital entrepreneurship. The chapter concludes with a case study about 'Chiara Ferragni', a successful Italian influencer and female digital international entrepreneur in the fashion industry.

Keywords Digital entrepreneurship • Female entrepreneurship • Digital platforms • Technology • Social media

© The Author(s), under exclusive license to Springer Nature Switzerland AG 2025
D. Kabbara, *Transformative Entrepreneurship in the Global Landscape*, https://doi.org/10.1007/978-3-031-77141-5_4

4.1 Digital Entrepreneurship

4.1.1 Digital Technologies' Role in the Entrepreneurial Context

Digital platforms, infrastructures, and technologies keep creating new business opportunities and enabling existing businesses to expand their offline operations into online ones. As a result, a new type of entrepreneurial activity known as "digital entrepreneurship" has emerged (Jafari-Sadeghi et al., 2021). Digital entrepreneurship is defined as "a subcategory of entrepreneurship in which some or all of what would be physical in a traditional organisation has been digitised" (Hull et al., 2007, p. 293). Additionally, the European Commission defined digital entrepreneurship as: 'Digital entrepreneurship embraces all new ventures and the transformation of existing businesses that drive economic and/or social value by creating and using novel digital technologies. Digital enterprises are characterised by a high intensity of utilisation of novel digital technologies (particularly social, big data, mobile and cloud solutions) to improve business operations, invent new business models, sharpen business intelligence, and engage with customers and stakeholders. They create jobs and growth opportunities for the future. The digital transformation will alter the entrepreneurial landscape, giving alternative financing sources reliant on Internet-based platforms a greater role and expanding market opportunities for aspiring business owners, including women. Innovation in technology has a big influence on the growing market for entrepreneurial ventures in the service industry. This is particularly pertinent for small, entrepreneurial businesses because they must use technology to overcome their resource shortage because they face the liability of newness and smallness

Digital transformation refers to the integration of digital technology into all areas of a business, fundamentally changing how you operate and deliver value to customers. This global perspective emphasises how innovative, culturally sensitive, and adaptable entrepreneurs are necessary to maintain competitiveness and promote digital entrepreneurship on a global scale.

Digital technologies shape the entrepreneurial ecosystem and are considered a major source of transformation in the entrepreneurial environment (Jafari-Sadeghi et al., 2021). According to (Kraus et al., 2018), the startup ecosystem is undergoing a transformation due to the emergence of new technology and applications, which is expanding the opportunities for business owners and entrepreneurs.

The way we live, and work has changed as a result of the wide range of digital technologies, platforms, and infrastructures that have emerged recently. Entrepreneurial businesses founded by men and women in nearly every industry have been compelled to investigate cutting-edge technology and its applications and frequently have no choice but to adopt them. This process has frequently resulted in the modification of important business operations, which has an impact on the founders' decisions to alter their concepts and management structures as well as their products and services.

4.1.2 Digital Platforms as Catalysts for Change

Digital technologies and platforms are a crucial catalyst for change in the entrepreneurial landscape and present more chances for prospective business owners, particularly women. Women entrepreneurs are becoming more and more involved in digital entrepreneurship as a result of time and technology advancements (Ughetto et al., 2020). Digital firms are facing new opportunities and challenges as a result of the revolution in the entrepreneurial landscape brought about by digital technologies (Jafari-Sadeghi et al., 2021). Additionally, the digital revolution of Industry 4.0 is driving businesses and entrepreneurs to seek technical innovation (Denicolai et al., 2021). The increasing use of mobile internet and information and computing technologies (ICTs) in recent years has enhanced the potential for online entrepreneurship. The Internet has emerged as a potent instrument for initiating new business ventures and boosting operational effectiveness. Research on this topic is greatly aided by studying the effects of digital transformation on value creation at the national level, especially when viewed through the prism of the dynamic capabilities that support the adoption of digital innovation, such as technological entrepreneurship and technological market expansion. The digital revolution creates a variety of chances for entrepreneurship, which has been demonstrated to result in the creation of value at the local, regional, and national levels. Because of the internet and technological advancements, businesses can now continuously expand their market by lowering the cost of looking for new opportunities.

According to Kraus et al. (2019), there has been a discernible change in the manner in which entrepreneurs carry out their business operations as a result of digital transformation. This change is evident in six main areas that have been extensively discussed in the literature: digital business models, digital entrepreneurship process, digital ecosystems, platform strategies, social, digital entrepreneurship, and entrepreneurship education.

For instance, the emergence of Industry 4.0 and the proliferation of various new digital industrial technologies—such as the Internet of Things, big data analytics, robotics, and advanced manufacturing methods—are among the developments resulting from these digital technologies. According to (Strange & Zucchella, 2017), these digital tools optimise production costs and quality while facilitating device interactions and communications. Furthermore, the rise of social media and artificial intelligence is thought to be one of the main forces behind business expansion and has provided companies and entrepreneurs with a more effective and straightforward means of connecting with customers in both domestic and international markets. They can provide improved sustainability impacts (Lammers et al., 2022), increased flexibility (Zaheer et al., 2022), and international expansion (Sinkovics et al., 2013). Additionally, financial digital platforms (Groza et al., 2020), digital platforms for education (Fu et al., 2021), and e-learning online platforms (Alexe & Alexe, 2019) are regarded as essential instruments for promoting inclusive international entrepreneurship among all groups, including women, minorities, and people with disabilities. According to (Hsieh & Wu, 2019) digital platform is an online resource that facilitates communication and information sharing between businesses and individuals. These platforms have created new environments that may foster entrepreneurship.

4.2 Digital Inclusion

4.2.1 The Role of Technology to Promote Female (Inclusive) Entrepreneurship

As a result of the emergence and growth of digital platforms, women who experience a range of forms of discrimination and exclusion can now engage virtually and trade goods and services, creating new opportunities for empowerment and inclusion (Fu et al., 2021). Due to stereotypically defined technophobic attitudes, women used computers at a lower rate than men in the early 1990s. According to (Chang et al., 2016) women, particularly female entrepreneurs, now have more flexible options thanks to digital opportunities, which enable them to overcome obstacles related to paying for employment by starting their digital businesses. Because they are mostly in charge of taking care of their families and taking care of the home, female entrepreneurs have less time to develop their skills or succeed in extremely demanding technological roles. As a result, they look for simple and accessible digital tools to start their businesses. For instance, they can start unofficial home-based businesses using ICT, overcoming time and location constraints (Walker et al., 2008).

Digital technology, especially the internet, is thought to be an essential tool for knowledge acquisition, promoting the expansion of new digital businesses, and influencing entrepreneurship. In the digital economy, there are numerous crossing difficulties to gender parity. Gender inequality in the digital economy has historically led to challenges with digital expertise, internet access, and undesirable experiences on the internet. Gender digital equality, especially in emerging countries, continues to be hampered by a range of barriers to access, including affordability and skill. This can be particularly true for vulnerable and female informal entrepreneurs starting their own businesses in developing countries, like female entrepreneurs with low levels of education and managerial skills and living in countries with gender gap employment and economic crises. For instance, some female entrepreneurs work in the informal economy and take advantage of the benefits offered by the digital economy. Even if they have simple technological equipment and low managerial skills, female entrepreneurs struggle to be included in the business world and undertake informal entrepreneurial activities. They engage in digital subsistence entrepreneurial activities on social media without adhering to any regulations or formal rules (Delacroix et al., 2019; Salvi et al., 2023). In the informal economy, digital technology—primarily online sources—is viewed as a vital tool that influences decisions to participate in the informal economy, fosters the growth of informal firms in Zambia, and helps acquire knowledge (Tang & Konde, 2021). Furthermore, the authors of a recent study on the economies of Sub-Saharan Africa noted that the relationship between business formality and technological innovation enhances business productivity (Ndzana & Mvogo, 2024). Early-stage reduced competition, and trailing regulations are factors that draw new innovations and technologies to the informal economy. Other researchers looked at the informal manufacturing sector in India and came up with the idea of a "modern" informal business for companies that use more advanced technology and are more productive (Shekar & Nataraj, 2023).

The gendered gap in technology is widely viewed as the inevitable outcome of the social and cultural context. For instance, in the association of southeast Asian Nations inform (ASEAN) countries for example, the gender digital divide is primarily caused by a lack of device management, skill discrepancies, and an apparent or actual lack of advantages resulting from ICT adoption (Kabbara, 2024). Women have a shorter time to improve their abilities or to be successful in highly challenging technological roles, even at the CEO stage, because they are primarily responsible for unpaid domestic duties and family care.

4.2.2 Female Entrepreneurial Opportunities in the Digital Economy

The widespread adoption of information and computing technologies (ICTs) and mobile internet in recent years has increased entrepreneurial potential through online means and expanded the options for startups and entrepreneurs (Kabbara, 2024; Kraus et al., 2019). Because these technologies are more accessible and less expensive for smaller businesses as well (Baur & Wee, 2015), they can offer these businesses new tools and strategies for connecting with customers throughout the world as well as novel approaches to managing their operations and budgets.

Consequently, various types of entrepreneurs who implemented digitalisation in their businesses emerged. In recent literature, Brahem and Boussema (2023) proposed various categories of entrepreneurs who employed novel digital tools to launch their businesses. First, digital entrepreneurs offer services only online, requiring no physical presence; these services are cloud-based and rely heavily on big data. Second, social media entrepreneurs may have physical locations and channels of distribution in addition to marketing their goods and services and primarily interacting online (Brahem & Boussema, 2023). Social media entrepreneurs are defined as "Individuals or small firms that use their own or others' resources to create value by extracting opportunities via offering a service or product consisting of innovation in product/service characteristics, processes, distribution channels or places, or different innovative usage, to media market, or any other market which media is its main channel of interaction" (Khajeheian, 2012, p. 128). Social media entrepreneurs differ from the entrepreneurs involved in e-commerce. These later offer virtual stores, online tracking tools, search engines, and bank- or electronic-based payment systems on their websites. Social media entrepreneurs, on the other hand, do not require such an infrastructure. All they need to do is set up a profile on social media sites like Facebook, Instagram, and so on and market products to their followers (Virtanen et al., 2017). They have no record attesting to the payment's completion (Brahem & Boussema, 2023). Technology also offers a crucial tool for enhancing education in managerial and digital skills. In addition to online training and mentoring sessions, female informal entrepreneurs utilise e-learning platforms and participate in complimentary webinars. Particularly since the Covid pandemic, these digital platforms have grown in popularity (Ratten, 2023).

There is less "location" bound in the technological context when it comes to female informal entrepreneurship, according to the body of research on the subject. Without regard to a specific geographic area, technology can give women the chance to start and manage new unofficial businesses.

For female business owners, these technologies—particularly social media—are useful tools for improved networking and marketplace access, global client communication, and opportunity discovery (Beninger et al., 2016). More specifically, female entrepreneurs use social media platforms creatively to connect with people, unlike males, who are more inclined to use social media as a source of information. Additionally, women who use social media—including female entrepreneurs—tend to favour visual platforms like Pinterest, Instagram, and TikTok. In contrast, men tend to favour more text-focused channels (Gender-Specific Behaviours on Social Media and What They Mean for Online Communications (Atanasova, 2016).

Given the remoteness and the lack of physical infrastructure, social media and digital technologies can help (Female) entrepreneurs who have been excluded from economic development (Alekhina & Ganelli, 2021). Female entrepreneurs create online businesses and overcome the obstacles they face using Internet technologies (Brahem & Boussema, 2023; Ughetto et al., 2020). Other authors highlighted the importance of technology in the global expansion of female entrepreneurs. For instance, Pergelova et al. (2019) described how technological advancements can democratise entrepreneurship by improving communication with partners and clients and providing access to information about global markets.

Previous literature studied women's participation in digital entrepreneurship in developing nations with rigorous cultural and social norms. The authors have examined women's perceptions of digital technology within the framework of cyberfeminism research, highlighting the internet's disruptive potential in lowering barriers to entrepreneurship for a historically affected group.

Digital opportunities provide women with flexible options that allow them to overcome hurdles in paying for employment by becoming digital entrepreneurs. examined women's involvement in digital entrepreneurship in developing countries with rigid cultural and social conventions. In the framework of cyberfeminism research, the authors have looked at how women perceive digital technology, underlining the disruptive potential of the internet in removing hurdles to entrepreneurship for a population that has traditionally been marginalised in the field. Due to a lack of physical infrastructure and remoteness, digital commerce and digital entrepreneurship can assist in integrating people who have been kept out of economic development (Alekhina & Ganelli, 2021). Similarly, Ughetto et al. (2020) examined the importance of gender in digital entrepreneurship. They described how women entrepreneurs build online businesses and overcome the obstacles they encounter by using internet technologies. Other authors have also emphasised the impact of digital technologies on the international expansion of female entrepreneurs (Pergelova et al., 2019). According to the authors, the advances in technology can democratise entrepreneurship by enhancing contact with clients and partners and offering access to knowledge about international markets. Several authors have emphasised the significance of social media as a helpful tool for female business owners. Social media provides better access to networks and marketplaces, communicating with clients worldwide, and finding new opportunities.

4.3 Impact of Digital Technologies on Female Entrepreneurship

Digital technologies have driven changes in female entrepreneurs' attitudes and assisted in overcoming the obstacles they encounter (Martin & Tiu Wright, 2005; Martinez Dy et al., 2018). Recent authors emphasised the value of social media and digital platforms as helpful tools for individuals and groups looking to advance their own professional and personal development (Ditta-Apichai et al., 2024).

4.3.1 Business Impact

Female entrepreneurs leverage new digital technologies and the internet to launch and develop their new ventures (Brahem & Boussema, 2023; Ughetto et al., 2020). Digital work has enormous potential for creating employment opportunities for the marginalised labour force, especially for minorities, women and migrants -who were previously excluded from the labour force- due to the low entry barriers and the increased flexibility of work (Rani & Furrer, 2021). The paragraphs below illustrate how female entrepreneurs can employ digital technologies to overcome the barriers they face and launch their digital startups, hence impact their business. In France, as in other developed nations, certain scholars emphasised the importance of digital platforms for low-income female digital entrepreneurs (Delacroix et al., 2019). These authors asserted that poor French moms are using the free communication costs on social media sites like Facebook to their advantage as they engage in digital subsistence entrepreneurial activities against official regulations. By decreasing unemployment and creating new economic opportunities, these DTs help socially marginalised women who are female informal entrepreneurs participate in the economy more (Cesaroni et al., 2017; Crittenden et al., 2019).

First, to improve their economic status, female entrepreneurs can leverage digital technologies and mainly social media platforms to promote their products, build a strong image, attract followers and generate revenues. Taking advantage of the free communication costs on these platforms (Brahem & Boussema, 2023). For instance, female entrepreneur working in the crafting industry and handcrafts—those who create craft projects in their homes or home studios—are becoming increasingly recognised as part of a movement that supports small-scale, locally produced handmade goods, particularly in light of the economic uncertainty in their nation and the effects of climate change on a global scale. In the market for handicrafts (handmade jewellery, pottery, knitting and crafting, craft design cakes, etc.), female entrepreneurs can easily take pictures with their smartphones and make videos using a few simple, free applications (Canvas, Cap cut, Kapwing, Animoto, etc.). They promote their products on social media platforms (like TikTok, Instagram, Snapchat, Pinterest, YouTube Channel, etc.). Within a few months, they will be able to generate revenues. More specifically, female entrepreneurs use social media platforms creatively, favouring visual platforms to connect with people, unlike males, who are more inclined to use social media as a source of information. Similarly, the digital platform ecosystem and business model have created new avenues for people, mostly women, to work in other sectors of the housing and hospitality industries (Fu et al., 2021). A growing number of female entrepreneurs are employed by digital peer-to-peer rental platforms such as Airbnb, where they rent out their homes or clean rooms, for example.

Second, in order to address the shortage of financial capital, female entrepreneurs leverage digital technologies because they provide an alternate source of funding (as opposed to more traditional sources like banks) based on internet-based platforms. For example, female entrepreneurs rely on the internet to raise funds to finance their startups through digital financial platforms such as crowdfunding platforms (Groza et al., 2020) (like IndieGoGo, Kickstarter, etc....) or specialised crowdfunding sites just for female entrepreneurs (such as IFundWomen), which provide them access to debt-free capital(Groza et al., 2020).

4.3.2 Personal Impact

Digital platforms and technologies also affect female digital entrepreneurs on an individual or personal level.

First, to face the problem of family responsibility and work-life balance (Agarwal & Lenka, 2015), female entrepreneurs can benefit from digital technologies by providing them with more flexible work schedules and fewer restrictions on their mobility. Particularly, female entrepreneurs, mainly mothers, are mostly in charge of taking care of their families and homes and have less time to manage physical work. As a result, they look for simple and accessible digital tools to start their businesses and start unofficial home-based businesses, overcoming time and location constraints (Walker et al., 2008). Given the remoteness and the lack of physical infrastructure of these digital platforms, digital technologies can help female entrepreneurs who have been excluded from economic development (Alekhina & Ganelli, 2021).

Second, to face the obstacle of low education and managerial skills, female entrepreneurs leverage online e-learning platforms (such as LinkedIn Learning, Udemy, SkillShare, Coursera,.) and attend free webinars (such as Women's Business Development Center Webinars, LAEDA Women's Business Center Webinars, Let's Talk Business,...) in addition to online training and mentoring sessions. These digital platforms have become more popular, particularly after the COVID-19 pandemic (Ratten, 2023) and offer a vital tool for enhancing digital skills.

Third, the internet and 'cyberspace' can be emancipatory tools for women who pursue entrepreneurship. Previous literature, within the framework of cyberfeminism research, has examined women's perceptions of digital technology (Ughetto et al., 2020). The authors have highlighted the significant role of the internet and digital technologies in lowering the barriers to entrepreneurial entry (Martin & Tiu Wright, 2005). Other authors have investigated the emancipatory potential that digital entrepreneurship offers to women as a group that has historically been underrepresented in entrepreneurship (McAdam et al., 2020). According to McAdam et al. (2020), female entrepreneurs engage in digital entrepreneurship to 'transform their embodied selves and lived realities rather than to escape gender embodiment as offered by the online environment' (ibid., p. 1).

The interaction of female entrepreneurs in digital technologies, especially in social media, improves their capacity for expression, increases the amount of experience women share, and increases the degree to which they feel empowered to face and transform their challenging circumstances (Crittenden et al., 2019). The rise and expansion of digital platforms have made it possible for women, who face various forms of exclusion and discrimination, to interact virtually and exchange goods and services, opening up new possibilities for inclusion and empowerment (Fu et al., 2021).

As a result of technological advances, mainly social media, new means of online communication (e.g., blogs, microblogs, forums, chat rooms, and social networking sites) have contributed to empowering female entrepreneurship. 'Influencers' are individuals who disproportionately impact the spread of information or some related behaviour of interest (Bakshy et al., 2011, p. 66). According to Wiedmann et al. (2010), social influencers are: "persons who tend to be interpersonal transmitters of information and have relative influence in their social systems"(Wiedmann et al., 2010, p. 144). A number of these bloggers and influencers later went on to start their own companies and pursue entrepreneurship. For instance, influencers leverage digital platforms to create digital content that leads potential buyers to interact with their company (Lee & Theokary, 2021; Wang et al., 2019). According to the Content Marketing Institute, "Content marketing is the marketing and Business Process for creating and distributing relevant and valuable content to attract, acquire, and engage a clearly defined and understood target audience—with the objective of driving profitable customer action" (Content Marketing Institute, 2015). Content marketing is considered a significant tool in generating sales. Influencer marketing is becoming more and more popular as an essential component of businesses' digital marketing strategies (Appel et al., 2020; Li et al., 2021). This is demonstrated by the market growth of global influencer marketing, which increased from $1.7 billion (USD) in 2016 to $13.8 billion in 2021 (Statista, 2021).

Therefore, as discussed above, the technological context facilitates integrative economic and social value creation and improves the connectivity between female entrepreneurs and their users (as clients) locally and globally (Kabbara, 2023). On a social level, it lessens their feelings of isolation, boosts their social capital, and enhances their social lives by allowing them to be a part of a larger social network (Cesaroni et al., 2017).

The entrepreneurial opportunity to launch a new digital business emerges from a complex pattern of changing conditions: female entrepreneurs' proficiency in an industry (fashion, food, technological advancements, political and financial crises, socio-cultural and economic circumstances, and an increase in the number of female social media users. Female entrepreneurs explored entrepreneurial opportunities at a certain point because of a juxtaposition of these conditions that did not previously exist (Baron, 2006). It appears that female entrepreneurs created a complementarity between the affordances of digital technologies within the value creation element and the values of the social logic (e.g., female user community development). They integrated various digital artefacts and infrastructures, establishing areas for collective engagement. They control the features of their business models in this digitally technological environment, making them more flexible and dynamic (Caputo et al., 2019).

4.4 Trade-off Technology on Female Digital Entrepreneurship

Research on technology in the context of entrepreneurship emphasises that there are negative aspects to technology as well as the potential for conflict. It might even prevent female entrepreneurship. Since they frequently create products that are less expensive, imitative, and/or have little to no technological content, female businesses may be wary of new technologies. Female entrepreneurs (especially in emerging countries) tend to adopt primarily technological solutions like digital platforms, search engines, and social media since they consider these platforms a source of revenue while working from home, particularly because of low costs and barriers to entry.

Second, hidden transactions may result in seizures, tax bills, and injunctions if discovered by the authorities due to certain online payment systems and software-based accounting systems that record transaction details (Pathak et al., 2016).

Third, female digital entrepreneurs may encounter conflicts and compromises when using social media and DTs for their business. First, the visibility/invisibility paradox (Nason et al., 2024) is more evident in these technological contexts: these women work in the shadow economy but may post about their goods and services on social media in an attempt to reach customers outside of their limited social and geographic context. "Limited resources, the need for new digital skills, digital stress because of the demand for online presence, and scanning and maintenance of social media" are additional factors contributing to tensions in the digital context (Olsson & Bernhard, 2021, p. 378). Women entrepreneurs may face difficulties in using IT and problems related to internet coverage.

Fourth, female digital entrepreneurs may face a risk of entrepreneurial burnout. This later is influenced by their business ventures, their personalities, and their reliance on social media (Palmer et al., 2021). Additionally, female entrepreneurs in digital markets have to deal with the negative aspects of social media discourse. More precisely, according to Tunio et al. (2023), young female entrepreneurs are more likely to become targets of cyberbullying and online harassment from their online networks. On their social media profiles, they might also receive aggressive and hostile remarks about their products, which could harm their reputation online (Sawy & Bögenhold, 2023). Anxiety and stress levels can rise in female entrepreneurs who are frequently subjected to disparaging remarks. They might feel overpowered by the negativity they've already encountered or fear experiencing more of it online. Additionally, over time, these disparaging remarks have the potential to erode their self-esteem and contribute to feelings of sadness and depression. Perceived online communication reflects the act or the degree of consumption that an individual perceives over receiving positive or negative messages online from any former customer in general and from social media influencers in particular. In fact, digital inclusion is hampered by concerns about online security and safety. For instance, a large amount of cyberbullying is directed toward prominent women activists, young women, religious minorities, and others.

In addition, earlier research on technology in the context of entrepreneurship has shown that there are conflicts and disadvantages with technology and that it may even prevent (female) informal entrepreneurship. From the standpoint of the informal economy, informal businesses create cheaper goods due to a lack of resources and a low level of technology (Ndzana & Mvogo, 2024). The costs of informality that new businesses must pay early on diminish their drive and ability to innovate. As a result, these businesses produce new goods that are more similar to the original. Furthermore, concealed transactions may result in tax bills if discovered by the authorities due to certain online payment systems and software-based accounting systems that record transaction details (Pathak et al., 2016).

Lastly, it should be emphasised that female entrepreneurs can have some influence on the technological context in addition to how the technological context affects them (both favourably and unfavourably). For instance, female entrepreneurs who use DTs to publicly share their accomplishments may be viewed as role models by women who are marginalised and under-represented, and they may also help shape the possibilities available on digital platforms. Female entrepreneurs may feel more confident about taking steps towards expanding their businesses as a result of their growing online presence.

4.5 Case Study of an Influencer as a Female International Digital Entrepreneur in the Fashion Industry

Chiara Ferragni Brand was selected as a case study subject because she is an Italian woman who is a social media influencer in the fashion industry. The most well-known Italian fashion blogger, who later became a businesswoman, has a substantial social media following, has launched her own clothing line, and has led several brand partnerships (such as Louis Vuitton). This case was chosen as an appropriate example to examine how a blogger and influencer used social media and digital platforms to become a well-known global female entrepreneur. Chiara Ferragni served as a mediator in the relationship between the customer and the brand as an influencer and fashion blogger. Through her blogging, she was able to acquire more influencers over consumers as an intermediary than fashion brands can have on their own.

CHIARA FERRAGNI BRAND
Chiara Ferragni launched her blog, The Blonde Salad, in 2009 while attending Milan's Bocconi University for a degree in law. She is the CEO of TBS CREW Srl and Chiara Ferragni brand and is part of the board of billionaire Diego Della Valle's fashion company, Tod's Group.

Initially indicative of the "mixed salad" of interests, including travel, beauty and food, the blog has since become focused on fashion. Among her style choices and inspirations, The Blonde Salad charts her collaborations with an impressive roster of design houses, including Dior, Louis Vuitton, Ermenegildo Zegna, Benetton and Mango. She has also been on the cover of fashion and business magazines all over the world, including Vogue, The New York Times, Vanity Fair and Harper's Bazaar. She was also announced as the European ambassador of Amazon Fashion and face of its Spring 2016.

Ferragni's namesake line, Chiara Ferragni Collection, started out in 2013 as a footwear line with Luisa Via Roma. It has since expanded into clothing, accessories and children's wear and boasts four flagship stores and over 300 retail doors. The company reported 2016 revenues of €17 million ($20 million).

In June 2023, venture firm AVM Gestioni reportedly bought 25 percent of Ferragni's company Fenice, at a €75 million valuation.

In September 2023, Ferragni joined the Camera Moda Fashion Trust Board as a member of the Advisory Committee.

Source: BusinessofFashion.com website

Chiara Ferragni is a well-known influential figure. She began her career as an amateur fashionista and has since become a successful fashion blogger and businesswoman. In fact, Ferragni's blog has grown to have about 29 million Instagram followers after only 15 years of publication, and it has since become a popular lifestyle publication. Ferragni was able to upend the conventional wisdom in the fashion industry and establish herself as a key player. She managed to go from being an amateur fashionista to a successful fashion entrepreneur and icon.

In addition to her outstanding accomplishments, Chiara has also paved the way for aspiring female entrepreneurs in the fashion industry to become fashion industry entrepreneurs.

(continued)

> (continued)
>
> Founded in 2013 as a pop-inspired fashion footwear brand, the concept originated with CEO, creative director, and muse Chiara Ferragni. The brand changed in a matter of seasons to include shoes, apparel, and accessories that are all distinguished by the iconic eye-shaped logo.
>
> With the opening of pop-up locations at Le Bon Marché in Paris, LuisaViaRoma in Florence, Apropos in Cologne, Breeze Centre in Taiwan, and Selfridges in London, the brand made its first moves towards international expansion in 2016.
>
> With the opening of flagship locations in the centre of the trendiest cities—Milan, Paris, Shanghai, and Hong Kong—the brand has grown stronger since July 2017.
>
> Source: ChiaraFerragnibrand.com website

Blogging is becoming more and more regarded as a way to get into the fashion industry and establish a personal brand. Since its 2013 launch as a fashion shoe company, Chiara Ferragni has successfully expanded into a number of other product categories, such as clothing, accessories, and jewellery. As a result, it is currently leading the rapidly expanding field of fashion blogger and entrepreneur brands. The brand, which is well-known for its "Flirting" motif, now offers fashionable yet playful collections that draw inspiration from pop culture, music, travel, and the world of contemporary art.

According to a previous interview with Chiara Ferragni published in the Financial Times by Rachel Sanderson (February 8, 2019), Chiara, who was born in Milan, began writing on her blog in both Italian and English when she was a 15-year-old law student at the university. She launched her own website in 2010 to sell clothing and accessories both online and through pop-up shops and flagships in Paris, Milan, and China. She left the university just a few exams short of graduating, never finishing her degree. She departed for the United States in 2013. She desired to become fluent in English and have a global sense of identity. Forbes nominated her for its '30 under 30' list. After three years, she made the decision to return home and turn to Italy, where she (at the time) had 17 million European followers. She worked with international companies like Intimissimi, Dior, and Lancôme. Chiara received a nomination for the LVMH Prize ambassadorship and launched the Beauty Bites online beauty masterclass project. She started a new line of stylish streetwear. She worked with Emily Weiss, a former Vogue fashion assistant and the creator of the millennial online beauty brand. It was thanks to this partnership that she was able to secure venture capital funding.

She uses her mother and sisters, in particular, as business partners to market and support her brands online.

After two years, she turned down a job offer from Berlosconi's media company because she wanted to work as a TV fashion reporter. She insisted on keeping her fame and reputation at the Italian national level and refused to work in the media. She has a global vision, hopes to expand internationally, and wants to draw in more foreign customers and collaborators. However, she has faced backlash from the public on social media. However, she knew how to handle it and chose to move forward despite people spreading hate and trying to undermine her. She shared a lot of moments with her fans of her family and children, posting nearly six times a day. She consistently uses digital channels to be open and accessible to her consumers.

From this example, successful digital women entrepreneurs must overcome a number of challenges and setbacks. Chiara has always had a determination, passion, and a global vision for digital entrepreneurship. When Chiara made networks with another famous fashion assistant, her business began to grow and attracted venture capital.

As a digital entrepreneur, she always receives criticism; she always manages to be calm and remain resilient and flexible; these negative comments are considered a motivation for her.

This case demonstrates that the motivation behind digital entrepreneurship is the need to follow a passion for being a digital fashion international entrepreneur; she moved to another continent, and then she felt she needed to turn back home after getting an international reputation in the fashion industry. She was able to reach a broad audience of customers by doing this and promoting herself as an influencer. This is how she was able to cope with her liability of newness, highlighting the importance of partnerships in the companies' internationalisation process. A key element in her success was her passion for being a fashion entrepreneur and not to limit herself as an influencer who promotes other companies' brands. It's interesting to observe that, in this instance, networking and determination mitigate the liabilities of newness and smallness.

The female digital entrepreneur's family—mainly her sisters and mother— who became her partners in a later phase- turned out to be important in encouraging and inspiring her to promote her brands through digital platforms. Hence, her family (and husband at a certain period) acts as the central support system for the (international) digital entrepreneurial process and enables Chiara to progressively become acknowledged as a successful female digital entrepreneur.

REFERENCES

Agarwal, S., & Lenka, U. (2015). Study on work-life balance of women entrepreneurs–review and research agenda. *Industrial and Commercial Training*.

Alekhina, V., & Ganelli, G. (2021). Determinants of inclusive growth in ASEAN. *Journal of the Asia Pacific Economy*, 1–33.

Alexe, C.-G., & Alexe, C.-M. (2019). E-learning-facilitator tool for the development of technological entrepreneurship. *eLearning & Software for Education, 2*.

Appel, G., Grewal, L., Hadi, R., & Stephen, A. T. (2020). The future of social media in marketing. *Journal of the Academy of Marketing Science, 48*(1), 79–95.

Atanasova, A. (2016). Gender-specific behaviors on social media and what they mean for online communications.

Bakshy, E., Hofman, J. M., Mason, W. A., & Watts, D. J. (2011). *Everyone's an influencer: Quantifying influence on twitter*. Paper presented at the Proceedings of the fourth ACM international conference on Web search and data mining.

Baron, R. A. (2006). Opportunity recognition as pattern recognition: How entrepreneurs "connect the dots" to identify new business opportunities. *Academy of Management Perspectives, 20*(1), 104–119.

Baur, C., & Wee, D. (2015). Manufacturing's next act. *McKinsey & Company, 6*, 1–5.

Beninger, S., Ajjan, H., Mostafa, R. B., & Crittenden, V. L. (2016). A road to empowerment: Social media use by women entrepreneurs in Egypt. *International Journal of Entrepreneurship and Small Business, 27*(2–3), 308–332.

Brahem, M., & Boussema, S. (2023). Social media entrepreneurship as an opportunity for women: The case of Facebook-commerce. *The International Journal of Entrepreneurship and Innovation, 24*(3), 191–201.

Caputo, A., Fiorentino, R., & Garzella, S. (2019). From the boundaries of management to the management of boundaries: Business processes, capabilities and negotiations. *Business Process Management Journal, 25*(3), 391–413.

Cesaroni, F. M., Demartini, P., & Paoloni, P. (2017). Women in business and social media: Implications for female entrepreneurship in emerging countries. *African Journal of Business Management, 11*(14), 316–326.

Chang, J.-H., Rynhart, G., & Huynh, P. (2016). *ASEAN in transformation: Textiles, clothing and footwear: Refashioning the future*. ILO Geneva.

Content Marketing Institute. (2015). *What Is Content Marketing?*. Retrieved on 25 June 2024 from http://contentmarketinginstitute.com/what-is-content-marketing/.

Crittenden, V. L., Crittenden, W. F., & Ajjan, H. (2019). Empowering women micro-entrepreneurs in emerging economies: The role of information communications technology. *Journal of Business Research, 98*, 191–203.

Delacroix, E., Parguel, B., & Benoit-Moreau, F. (2019). Digital subsistence entrepreneurs on Facebook. *Technological Forecasting and Social Change, 146*, 887–899.

Denicolai, S., Zucchella, A., & Magnani, G. (2021). Internationalization, digitalization, and sustainability: Are SMEs ready? A survey on synergies and substituting effects among growth paths. *Technological Forecasting and Social Change, 166*, 120650.

Ditta-Apichai, M., Gretzel, U., & Kattiyapornpong, U. (2024). Platform empowerment: Facebook's role in facilitating female micro-entrepreneurship in tourism. *Journal of Sustainable Tourism, 32*(3), 540–559.

Fu, X., Avenyo, E., & Ghauri, P. (2021). Digital platforms and development: A survey of the literature. *Innovation and Development, 11*(2–3), 303–321.

Groza, M. P., Groza, M. D., & Barral, L. M. (2020). Women backing women: The role of crowdfunding in empowering female consumer-investors and entrepreneurs. *Journal of Business Research, 117*, 432–442.

Hsieh, Y.-J., & Wu, Y. J. (2019). Entrepreneurship through the platform strategy in the digital era: Insights and research opportunities. *Computers in Human Behavior, 95*, 315–323.

Hull, C. E., Hung, Y.-T. C., Hair, N., Perotti, V., & DeMartino, R. (2007). Taking advantage of digital opportunities: A typology of digital entrepreneurship. *International Journal of Networking and Virtual Organisations, 4*(3), 290–303.

Jafari-Sadeghi, V., Garcia-Perez, A., Candelo, E., & Couturier, J. (2021). Exploring the impact of digital transformation on technology entrepreneurship and technological market expansion: The role of technology readiness, exploration and exploitation. *Journal of Business Research, 124*, 100–111.

Kabbara, D. (2023). Female entrepreneurship: Typologies, drivers and value creation. In *New horizons and global perspectives in female entrepreneurship research* (pp. 93–112). Emerald Publishing Limited.

Kabbara, D. (2024). Women's Entrepreneurship Policy: Enhancing Female Business Ownership in the Digital Era. In: Dana L-P and Chhabra M (eds) *Women Entrepreneurship Policy: Context, Theory, and Practice*, 125–150. Springer Nature Singapore.

Khajeheian, D. (2012). New venture creation in social media platform; Towards a framework for media entrepreneurship. In *Handbook of social media management: Value chain and business models in changing media markets* (pp. 125–142). Springer.

Kraus, S., Palmer, C., Kailer, N., Kallinger, F. L., & Spitzer, J. (2018). Digital entrepreneurship: A research agenda on new business models for the twenty-first century. *International Journal of Entrepreneurial Behavior & Research*.

Kraus, S., Palmer, C., Kailer, N., Kallinger, F. L., & Spitzer, J. (2019). Digital entrepreneurship: A research agenda on new business models for the twenty-first century. *International Journal of Entrepreneurial Behavior & Research, 25*(2), 353–375.

Lammers, T., Rashid, L., Kratzer, J., & Voinov, A. (2022). An analysis of the sustainability goals of digital technology start-ups in Berlin. *Technological Forecasting and Social Change, 185*, 122096.

Lee, M. T., & Theokary, C. (2021). The superstar social media influencer: Exploiting linguistic style and emotional contagion over content? *Journal of Business Research, 132*, 860–871.

Li, F., Larimo, J., & Leonidou, L. C. (2021). Social media marketing strategy: Definition, conceptualization, taxonomy, validation, and future agenda. *Journal of the Academy of Marketing Science, 49*, 51–70.

Martin, L. M., & Tiu Wright, L. (2005). No gender in cyberspace? Empowering entrepreneurship and innovation in female-run ICT small firms. *International Journal of Entrepreneurial Behavior & Research, 11*(2), 162–178.

Martinez Dy, A., Martin, L., & Marlow, S. (2018). Emancipation through digital entrepreneurship? A critical realist analysis. *Organization, 25*(5), 585–608.

McAdam, M., Crowley, C., & Harrison, R. T. (2020). Digital girl: Cyberfeminism and the emancipatory potential of digital entrepreneurship in emerging economies. *Small Business Economics, 55*, 349–362.

Nason, R., Vedula, S., Bothello, J., Bacq, S., & Charman, A. (2024). Sight unseen: The visibility paradox of entrepreneurship in an informal economy. *Journal of Business Venturing, 39*(2), 106364.

Ndzana, M. E., & Mvogo, P. G. (2024). Formality, innovation and entrepreneurial business performance in francophone Sub-Saharan Africa. *Journal of Small Business and Enterprise Development, 31*(2), 350–376.

Olsson, A. K., & Bernhard, I. (2021). Keeping up the pace of digitalization in small businesses–Women entrepreneurs' knowledge and use of social media. *International Journal of Entrepreneurial Behavior & Research, 27*(2), 378–396.

Palmer, C., Kraus, S., Kailer, N., Huber, L., & Öner, Z. H. (2021). Entrepreneurial burnout: A systematic review and research map. *International Journal of Entrepreneurship and Small Business, 43*(3), 438–461.

Pathak, S., Xavier-Oliveira, E., & Laplume, A. O. (2016). Technology use and availability in entrepreneurship: Informal economy as moderator of institutions in emerging economies. *The Journal of Technology Transfer, 41*, 506–529.

Pergelova, A., Manolova, T., Simeonova-Ganeva, R., & Yordanova, D. (2019). Democratizing entrepreneurship? Digital technologies and the internationalization of female-led SMEs. *Journal of Small Business Management, 57*(1), 14–39.

Rani, U., & Furrer, M. (2021). Digital labour platforms and new forms of flexible work in developing countries: Algorithmic management of work and workers. *Competition and Change, 25*(2), 212–236.

Ratten, V. (2023). Digital platforms and transformational entrepreneurship during the COVID-19 crisis. *International Journal of Information Management, 72*, 102534.

Salvi, E., Belz, F.-M., & Bacq, S. (2023). Informal entrepreneurship: An integrative review and future research agenda. *Entrepreneurship Theory and Practice, 47*(2), 265–303.

Sawy, A., & Bögenhold, D. (2023). Dark, darker, social media: Dark side experiences, identity protection, and preventive strategies of micro entrepreneurs on social media. *Journal of Research in Marketing and Entrepreneurship, 25*(2), 223–252.

Shekar, K. C., & Nataraj, M. (2023). Subcontracting and enterprise development in India's informal manufacturing sector. *Journal of Small Business and Enterprise Development, 30*(3), 448–474.

Sinkovics, N., Sinkovics, R. R., & "Bryan" Jean, R. J. (2013). The internet as an alternative path to internationalization? *International Marketing Review, 30*(2), 130–155.

Statista. (2021). Influencer Marketing Size Worldwide from 2016–2021. https://www.statista.com/statistics/1092819/global-influencer-market-size

Strange, R., & Zucchella, A. (2017). Industry 4.0, global value chains and international business. *Multinational Business Review*.

Tang, Y. K., & Konde, V. (2021). Which resource acquisition acts drive growth of informal firms? Evidence from Zambia. *Journal of Small Business and Enterprise Development, 28*(6), 888–907.

Tunio, M. N., Shaikh, E., Katper, N. K., & Brahmi, M. (2023). Nascent entrepreneurs and challenges in the digital market in developing countries. *International Journal of Public Sector Performance Management, 12*(1–2), 140–153.

Ughetto, E., Rossi, M., Audretsch, D., & Lehmann, E. E. (2020). Female entrepreneurship in the digital era. *Small Business Economics, 55*(2), 305–312.

Virtanen, H., Björk, P., & Sjöström, E. (2017). Follow for follow: Marketing of a start-up company on Instagram. *Journal of Small Business and Enterprise Development, 24*(3), 468–484.

Walker, E., Wang, C., & Redmond, J. (2008). Women and work-life balance: Is home-based business ownership the solution? *Equal Opportunities International, 27*(3), 258–275.

Wang, W.-L., Malthouse, E. C., Calder, B., & Uzunoglu, E. (2019). B2B content marketing for professional services: In-person versus digital contacts. *Industrial Marketing Management, 81*, 160–168.

Wiedmann, K.-P., Hennigs, N., & Langner, S. (2010). Spreading the word of fashion: Identifying social influencers in fashion marketing. *Journal of Global Fashion Marketing, 1*(3), 142–153.

Zaheer, H., Breyer, Y., Dumay, J., & Enjeti, M. (2022). The entrepreneurial journeys of digital start-up founders. *Technological Forecasting and Social Change, 179*, 121638.

CHAPTER 5

Sustainable Entrepreneurship: The Engagement of Female Entrepreneurs

Abstract Businesses are increasingly using transformative entrepreneurship for sustainability. It is a major revolution that is bringing new perspectives on sustainability through the development of new competencies and sustainable business models. Micro, small, and medium-sized business owners who are female have a great deal of potential for innovation and for reducing the consequences of climate change and environmental degradation. This chapter will address the term sustainable entrepreneurship and the motivation of female entrepreneurs to work in the circular economy. This chapter also highlights the trade-off of technology on female digital entrepreneurship. The chapter concludes with a case study about 'Chiara Ferragni', a successful Italian influencer and female digital international entrepreneur in the fashion industry.

Keywords Sustainable entrepreneurship • Born circular firm • Female sustainable entrepreneur • Circular business model • Female sustainable entrepreneur • SDGs

5.1 Transformative Entrepreneurship in Circular Economy and Sustainable Entrepreneurship

The term "sustainability" has become one of the most frequently used buzzwords over the last few years, and its use is constantly increasing (Apetrei et al., 2021). There are multiple definitions given in the literature, but the European Commission defines sustainability or sustainable development as "meeting the needs of the present whilst ensuring future generations can meet their own needs". Sustainability not only includes environmental issues but is a combination of three bases: environmental, social, and economic. Capra and Mattei (2015) stated that 'Sustainability is not an individual property but a property of an entire web of relationships, and it always involves a whole community'. The term sustainability was first mentioned by a German forester in his book, which explained the long-term maintenance of forests. However, it was not until the late 1960s and 1970s that the term sustainability gained wider attention. The terms "sustainability" and "circular economy" have gained traction in the field of environmental economics and management since the 1960s. This era saw the emergence of environmental awareness and the foundation of environmental NGOs and the Earth Day movement.

In the course of this movement, also businesses started to shift their focus. The 1990s saw the widespread acceptance of Corporate Social Responsibility (CSR), a business model that includes social and environmental concerns instead of only focusing on economic profits. Publications like Donna Wood's "Corporate Social Performance Revisited", which improved early CSR models, and Archie Carroll's "The Pyramid of Corporate Social Responsibility", both published in 1991, influenced this time.

In the 2000s, entrepreneurs also began to focus on creating businesses that balance economic, social and environmental goals. The rise of social enterprises and benefit corporations exemplified this trend, and the term Sustainable Entrepreneurship gained attention. The word sustainable entrepreneurship is a combination of sustainability and entrepreneurship, so entrepreneurship addresses the social, economic and environmental concerns of relevant stakeholders (Gast et al., 2017). Gibbs (2006) understands sustainable entrepreneurship as using creative destruction to drive the creation of a holistic economic-environmental-social system.

Because of the growing awareness of sustainability, the circular economy movement arose in the 2010s, providing a practical framework for sustainable entrepreneurship to operate.

Sustainable entrepreneurship is associated with the concept of "sustainable development" and "entrepreneurship" (Guan et al., 2020). Scholars define entrepreneurship from different perspectives, such as the characteristics of the entrepreneurial actor. It is widely recognised that entrepreneurship has the characteristics of spotting opportunities, taking risks, and creating solutions through creativity and innovativeness (Ardichvili et al., 2003; Greco & de Jong, 2017; Kuckertz & Wagner, 2010).

When producing goods and services, the organisational model followed mostly by society is linear. This means that resources are withdrawn, processed into products, used by the consumer, and then disposed of without taking environmental and social externalities into account (de Oliveira & Oliveira, 2023). The feasibility of this economic model was questioned as the international community became aware of the increasing scarcity of natural resources, and the concept of circular economy gained popularity. The term circular economy itself was coined by two environmental economists, David Pearce and Kerry Turner, in their book Economics of Natural Resources and the Environment in 1990 (Pearce & Turner, 1989). However, some foundational concepts that contribute to the circular economy framework have been present for some time, predating 1990. The concept of circular economy lies far in the past, in the concepts and workings of nature, specifically in the observation of physical phenomena and natural cycles. They describe it as the idea that waste, when appropriately treated, can be converted back into a resource, forming closed-loop cycles in the production and consumption chain. The Ellen MacArthur Foundation, a UK-based charity that promotes the concept of a circular economy, offers one of the most recognised definitions of circular economy: "The circular economy is a system where materials never become waste and nature is regenerated. In a circular economy, products and materials are kept in circulation through processes like maintenance, reuse, refurbishment, remanufacture, recycling, and composting. The circular economy tackles climate change and other global challenges, like biodiversity loss, waste, and pollution, by decoupling economic activity from the consumption of finite resources."

The foundation promotes integrating aspects of other related concepts into the circular approach, such as cradle-to-cradle and closed-loop supply chains (Bhattacharjee & Cruz, 2015). However, while these concepts share common goals, they also possess distinct characteristics. Using them interchangeably can lead to confusion and ambiguity in defining the concept of circular economy. Therefore, it is important to clearly define CE and distinguish it from these related frameworks.

The concept of the circular economy is expansive, yet it can be summarised into three fundamental principles (Ellen MacArthur Foundation). The first principle encourages the elimination of waste and pollution, enhancing designs and allowing materials to re-enter the economy after being used. The second principle includes circulating products while keeping materials at their highest use. This means taking the technical cycle of reusing, repairing, remanufacturing, and recycling, as well as the biological cycle of composting and anaerobic digestion, into account. The third principle highlights the importance of regenerating nature. When moving to a circular economy, natural processes should be enhanced, and resources should be regenerated rather than only extracted. Those principles are increasingly being used, and this is reflected in the rising numbers of circular enterprises and the adoption of circular business models (Zucchella & Urban, 2019). The European Commission in their EU Action Plan highlighted, "In a circular economy, the value of products and materials is maintained for as long as possible; waste and resource use are minimised, and resources are kept within the economy when a product has reached the end of its life, to be used again and again to create further value" (European Commission, 2018).

The circular economy is often seen as a new business model that promotes a sustainable economy and a healthier society. Businesses are part of a holistic system and must balance economic development with environmental protection as well as social interest while executing their tasks (MacArthur, 2013). The circular economy is built on regenerative systems, focusing on the creation of long-lasting products and processes and incorporating practices such as maintenance, repair, reuse, remanufacturing, reconditioning, and recycling (This approach suggests reimagining the entire lifecycle of production and consumption, from the initial concept and design through supply chain development, manufacturing, distribution, and ultimately, consumption and end-of-life management (Lacy & Rutqvist, 2016).

5.1.1 Circular Entrepreneurship

Building on the principles of sustainable entrepreneurship and the circular economy, circular entrepreneurship emerges as a specialised domain where entrepreneurs apply circular economy concepts to develop innovative business models. Circular entrepreneurship (Cullen & De Angelis, 2021) represents an essential aspect of a complex socioeconomic system that demands a reevaluation of relationships, patterns and context in a technical, political, legal or cultural way (Zucchella & Urban, 2019). By nature, the circular economy is inclusive and collaborative, which means developing various relationships inside and outside firms' organisations is a major responsibility of circular entrepreneurship. This approach entails "creating responsible enterprises," including not only legally registered businesses but also responsible organisations.

Circular entrepreneurship introduces a new concept of social responsibility among influential actors—primarily entrepreneurs and enterprises but also extends to other organisations and institutions (Zucchella & Urban, 2019). It emphasises the importance of collaborative efforts and the integration of sustainable practices across various sectors to drive the transition towards a circular economy. Circular entrepreneurship specifically involves the exploration and exploitation of opportunities within the circular economy domain. Since the circular economy is seen as a strategy to achieve sustainability outcomes, circular entrepreneurship is a form of sustainable entrepreneurship. Circular entrepreneurship is interconnected with other types of sustainable entrepreneurship, such as organic entrepreneurship, which focuses on health and well-being; green entrepreneurship, which emphasises climate and ecosystem preservation; and blue entrepreneurship, which concentrates on clean water and marine life.

Entrepreneurs are considered individuals who identify and leverage new opportunities through innovative combinations, resulting in new products, methods of production, sources of raw materials, markets, and new organisational forms. One of the primary responsibilities of entrepreneurs is wealth creation, which involves producing goods and services, fostering innovations, and contributing to knowledge development, ultimately adding value to humankind (Zucchella & Urban, 2014). In the context of the circular economy, this added value comes from production processes designed to achieve "better with less" or "more with else" (Zucchella & Urban, 2019).

Although there has been significant discussion on sustainable development-oriented entrepreneurship over the past decade, more research and development are needed in the field (Kabbara et al., 2024). The transformation of entrepreneurship has emerged as the result of the transformation of the business model to the circular business model and the launch of a new type of firm, the 'born circular firm.'

5.1.2 Circular Business Model

The introduction of sustainability and circularity within existing businesses can lead to business model transformations. In particular, typologies of business model (BM) transformations toward sustainability have been outlined by Gauthier and Gilomen (2016) and are: business-as-usual, when no transformation occurs; business model adjustment, when transformation regards a single BM element; business model innovation, when major BM changes are implemented; business model redesign, when new value propositions result from a radical rethink of a BM.

The concept of a business model is comprehensively defined as "the activities and the resources which are at the foundation of the costs and revenues structure and create value for the diverse stakeholders" (Zucchella & Urban, 2019, p. 63). Scholars have also integrated the concept of business model into corporate sustainability research. Other authors propose that a business model for sustainability describes, analyses, manages, and communicates a company's sustainable value proposition to customers and stakeholders, how it creates and delivers this value, and how it captures economic value while maintaining or regenerating natural, social, and economic capital beyond organisational boundaries. The conceptualising of value can be broken down into core elements: value proposition (what value is offered and to whom), value creation (how value is exchanged or delivered), and value capture, forming a coherent whole.

In recent years, the definition of circular business models has evolved. A circular business model is, according to Lahti et al. (2018, p. 3) "designed to create and capture value while helping achieve an ideal state of resource usage." Galvão et al. (2020) conceptualise circular business models as business models that cycle, extend, intensify, and/or dematerialise material and energy loops to reduce resource inputs and minimise waste and emissions. This includes recycling measures (cycling), extending the use phase of products (extending), intensifying the use phase (intensifying), and substituting products with services and software solutions (dematerialising). Circular business models aim to reduce the environmental impact of economic activities, ideally achieving zero impact by closing resource loops.

Lüdeke-Freund et al. (2024) identify a range of circular business model design options supporting closed-loop material strategies, such as repair and maintenance, reuse and redistribution, refurbishment and remanufacturing, recycling, cascading and repurposing, and organic feedstock patterns. These models provide significant advantages in terms of customer value proposition and company value capture, including longer-lasting products, pay-per-use models, no waste handling at the end of product life, and upgradable products. Additionally, businesses benefit from additional revenue streams, long-term customer relationships, reduced material costs, improved reputation, and decreased material price volatility (Cullen & De Angelis, 2021).

Circular business models are categorised in circular startups into five archetypes: design-based, waste-based, platform-based, service-based, and nature-based models. Design-based models aim to improve resource usage efficiency, waste-based models extract value from unused waste streams, platform-based models facilitate resource sharing, service-based models offer product-service systems, and nature-based models offer products that reduce natural resource input. These categories are particularly relevant to the study of circular startups, emphasising the diversity and adaptability of circular business models in different business contexts.

Research by Zucchella and Urban (2019) identified several key characteristics of circular firms. Firstly, circular firms are not stand-alone entities but rely on a network of partners, consumers, communities, and institutions. Secondly, circular principles extend beyond manufacturing to service activities and agriculture, leading to the rise of circular service providers and new businesses that offer complementary assets and capabilities. Thirdly, circular principles often encompass social practices, such as employing disadvantaged individuals or ensuring fair wages and good working conditions. Fourthly, some firms innovate governance models to align with circular economy principles, adopting forms like benefit companies that emphasise purpose over profit maximisation. Lastly, the research distinguishes between established firms transitioning to circularity and young ventures "born circular." Young ventures may have an advantage due to their ability to design circular businesses from scratch, while large firms can provide significant impact and support for smaller enterprises, fostering mutual learning and growth.

The literature on circular business models emphasises the integration of circular principles into business models to create sustainable value. By adopting different strategies, companies can achieve both economic and ecological benefits. The evolution of circular business models reflects a broader understanding of sustainability, highlighting the importance of networked collaboration, social practices, and innovative governance in achieving circular economy goals.

5.1.3 Born Circular Firm

The concept of "born circular" firms is complexly linked with the evolving landscape of sustainable entrepreneurship, reflecting a paradigm shift towards integrating circular economy principles from the beginning of business ventures. Born-circular companies, as described by Zucchella and Urban (2019), are young ventures designed to deliver circular value propositions and explore circular economy opportunities. Born-circular companies contribute significantly to solving environmental issues by introducing new, environmentally sustainable products, services, and institutions.

Several design methods and tools for the development and implementation of circular business models exist in the literature. Some authors developed a framework that outlines a process of five phases (preparation, initiation, ideation, integration, and implementation). Other authors proposed 7P-model in order to understand and apply circularity within businesses: after a "prepare" phase in which companies establish the objective of sustainability and figure out both the circular economy basic principles and the scope of the change, firms then need to implement the Circular Economy in terms of processes, preservation, people, place, product and production and finally support the CE implementation mainly relying on team building and change management (Cullen & De Angelis, 2021). Additionally, the transition toward a CBM is also supported by the business model scan, which is a methodology consisting of a six-stage process related to value proposition, design, supply, manufacturing, use and next-life. In recent years, there has been a noticeable movement among established companies to adopt sustainability practices, and the rise of born-circular firms goes along with this movement. However, what sets born-circular companies apart is their inherent foundation on sustainability principles. These businesses, also referred to as "born-green" or "born-sustainable," are conceptualised with a strong emphasis on collaboration and innovation. Their processes and products are designed to be innovative and sustainable from the beginning, expressing a commitment to environmental, social, and economic sustainability (Ostermann et al., 2021).

Born-sustainable companies are distinguished by several key characteristics. Firstly, they are inherently aligned with principles of sustainability and social concern. Innovation is central to their operations, with a tendency for pioneering new technologies and disruptive innovations. They often operate in environments of uncertainty and risk. Born-circular start-ups, as observed by Cullen and De Angelis (2021), are characterised by their entrepreneurial drive to prevent waste and create community value, addressing both ecological and social dimensions throughout their business processes. Born circular or sustainable ventures are often for-profit businesses, so they need to make sure they can be profitable while sticking to circular economy principles. This does not appear to be problematic, as entrepreneurs have successfully established born circular firms by identifying profitable opportunities within the circular economy sector (Zucchella & Urban, 2019).

The business models of companies that are inherently designed to operate in a circular manner may vary. However, they can generally be categorised into three main groups: sharing/renting platforms, recycling/upcycling/extended product life, and services related to the circular economy. While the services themselves do not constitute a distinct business model, they can be viewed as a set of tasks aimed at providing essential support to the circular economy and enhancing the array of circular value propositions (Zucchella & Urban, 2019).

The motivation for founding born-circular firms frequently stems from a personal or professional recognition of environmental problems. These ventures not only address market limitations and regulatory structures but also enhance environmental awareness through their innovative business models and their newcomer status gives credibility to their claims of being part of the solution rather than contributors to environmental problems, a contrast to established companies attempting to rebrand themselves as sustainable. The motivation for launching a born circular firm will be discussed in the following sections.

5.2 Female Sustainable Entrepreneurship

Sustainable entrepreneurship considers entrepreneurship as a potential tool in moving both public and private socio-economic institutions toward a direction that promotes sustainable development (Tilley & Parrish, 2006).

Sustainable entrepreneurship has arisen as an overlapping research and practice area between entrepreneurship and sustainable development (Cohen & Winn, 2007). Female sustainable entrepreneurship is defined as "the process of discovering, evaluating, and exploiting economic opportunities that are present in market failures which detract from sustainability, including those that are environmentally relevant" (Dean & McMullen, 2007, p. 58). Several authors addressed the role of gender in sustainable entrepreneurship research (Criado-Gomis et al., 2020; Outsios & Farooqi, 2017). Other forms of female entrepreneurship emerged from sustainability phenomena. For instance, the term ecopreneur is defined as "an individual who creates green businesses to radically transform the economic sector in which he or she operates" (R. Isaak, 2016b, p. 71). Other authors defined these entrepreneurs as 'environmental entrepreneurs.' The latter is motivated by a desire to tackle environmental degradation (Dean & McMullen, 2007).

The growing relevance of sustainability in female entrepreneurship has garnered much interest in Management studies. Recently, several authors have pointed out that sustainability is a dynamic force behind many socio-economic developments (Barrachina Fernández et al., 2021) and a significant driver of productivity, growth, innovativeness and competitiveness for female entrepreneurs in the current economic environment (Debnath et al., 2019). The interdependence and the relations between sustainability awareness and sustainable behaviour, which underline the role of the individual on the firm level, have gained recent attention. Some scholars have addressed female femininity as a crucial impact on knowledge-intensive business services.

Sustainable entrepreneurship has arisen as an overlapping research and practice area between entrepreneurship and sustainable development (Cohen & Winn, 2007). Female sustainable entrepreneurship is defined as "the process of discovering, evaluating, and exploiting economic opportunities that are present in market failures which detract from sustainability, including those that are environmentally relevant" (Dean & McMullen, 2007, p. 58). Several authors addressed the role of gender in sustainable entrepreneurship research (Criado-Gomis et al., 2020; Outsios & Farooqi,

2017; Paolone et al., 2024). The growing relevance of sustainability in female entrepreneurship has garnered much interest in Management studies. Recently, several authors have pointed out that sustainability is a dynamic force behind many socioeconomic developments (Barrachina Fernández et al., 2021) and a significant driver of productivity, growth, innovativeness and competitiveness for female entrepreneurs in the current economic environment (Debnath et al., 2019). The interdependence and the relations between sustainability awareness and sustainable behaviour, which underline the role of the individual on the firm level, have gained recent attention. Some scholars have addressed female femininity as a crucial impact on knowledge-intensive business services.

Female entrepreneurs operate in many different industries, but they are often more attracted by ethical and environmental issues. Women in general have a higher motivation to become green as they are more involved with environmental concerns, the seriousness of environmental problems and their perceived responsibility compared to their male counterparts. Women, especially female entrepreneurs, are more engaged in green issues, leading them to find more sustainable businesses. The literature on women in sustainable entrepreneurship is still expandable and not yet fully developed, but recent studies, for example by Outsios and Farooqi (2017), show that women tend to contribute to global sustainability. The entrepreneurial research field grows in niches, and the female ecopreneurship niche is emerging. The term female ecopreneurship describes a female entrepreneur building their business on sustainability practices (Gunawan et al., 2021), trying to reach the largest audience possible, the masses of the market.

The presence of women in a company and the environmental sustainability of that business has only recently gained attention for analysis and empirical evidence in actual companies is still rare (Colombelli et al., 2024). For large companies and corporations, there is a lot of literature that analyses the representation of females on the board in the context of the adoption of sustainable practices. It is shown that companies with a high rate of women on their boards have higher corporate sustainability ratings as well as higher quality sustainability reports. Nevertheless, the same matter has almost not been analysed for startups, which would have been particularly interesting as the first stages of a company where the main values and mission are determined could be analysed. Colombelli et al. (2024), therefore, filled the gap by analysing "born green" companies and studying innovative startups in Italy. Their results showed that companies with a higher share of women are more likely to be social startups. Another dimension in literature is whether female entrepreneurs, in both MNEs and startups, adopt sustainability practices from the foundation of their businesses or if they transition to sustainability later in their operations. Some entrepreneurs may undergo a gradual shift toward sustainability, influenced by changing business opportunities, stakeholder expectations, societal and financial pressure, and the growing risk of legal disputes over climate change. Also, staying competitive is a great factor in the shift to sustainability. Ecopreneurship does not only include environmental issues but focuses on all aspects of sustainability, including social aspects. For instance, women would rather aim for social goals when doing business than pursue economic goals. Furthermore, female entrepreneurs focus more on objectives that may include promoting fair wages, addressing gender pay disparities, and prioritising local development over international expansion.

Ambepitiya (2016) conducted a survey of female entrepreneurs from four developing countries and found their business models centring around "trading with the poor, helping the community to develop skills and abilities, paying fair prices and receiving fair payments, encouraging fair treatment of all staff and encouraging environment-friendly conditions in business operations" (p. 176). Debnath et al. (2019) have been researching the role of women entrepreneurship in achieving the Sustainable Development Goals in Bangladesh, and their results showed that women entrepreneurs have the most significant influence on the SDG Gender Equality, as they can reduce inequalities by creating employment as well as improving women's decision-making capacity. MUO et al. (2023) looked at the influence of women's entrepreneurship on the SDGs in Nigeria and showed that women's entrepreneurship reduces poverty in the respective countries (Fig. 5.1).

According to the GEM report (2023), approximately 40% of global entrepreneurs stated that they take social and environmental sustainability into account when making business decisions; women do so somewhat more frequently than men. Additionally, compared to men, women entrepreneurs were more likely to report placing a higher priority on sustainability than on financial goals.

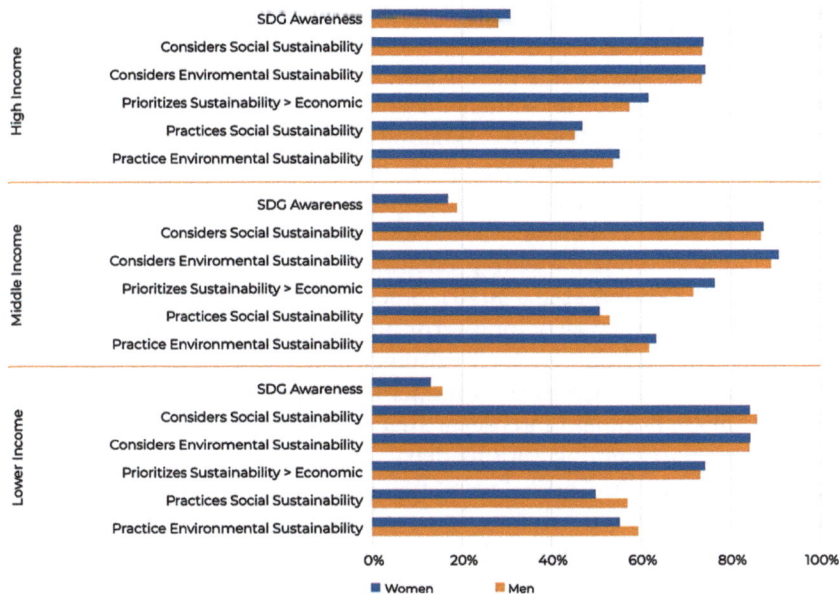

Fig. 5.1 Sustainability awareness, priorities, and practices for entrepreneurs by gender. (*Source*: Global Entrepreneurship Monitor (GEM) 2022/2023 Women's Entrepreneurship Report: Challenging Bias and Stereotypes. https://www.gem-consortium.org/file/open?fileId=51352)

5.3 Exploring the Motivations for Female Entrepreneurs to Engage in Circular Economy

Even though there is little literature on women entrepreneurs' reasons for starting born circular firms, numerous studies have delved into the motivations of entrepreneurs in adopting sustainable business practices.

In general, drivers of ecopreneurship practices can be classified into intrinsic and extrinsic motivations. Intrinsic drivers arise from internal stimuli, motivating individuals through personal values, beliefs, and internal rewards. Extrinsic drivers are provided by external agents, including societal pressures and rewards. Female sustainable entrepreneurs show a combination of prosocial motivation (Omoto & Snyder, 2010) and intrinsic (Amabile, 1997) to undertake entrepreneurial activities. They are motivated by self-fulfilment (Buttner & Moore, 1997), and driven by the desire to contribute to the environment and the planet (Criado-Gomis et al., 2020). The generation of social and economic value is inextricably linked to the creation of environmental value. When creating and producing their products, female sustainable entrepreneurs paid greater attention to using sustainable practices. While attempting to do no harm to the world, female entrepreneurs paid particular attention to using natural fabrics in their products and followed a waste minimisation practice (Dean & McMullen, 2007). Female sustainable entrepreneurs addressed more social and environmental entrepreneurial goals than economic entrepreneurial goals (Vuorio et al., 2018). Since they have several goals (people and the planet), they view long-term financial success as a necessary but not sufficient condition for their existence (Zucchella & Urban, 2019).

Internal factors such as the founder's entrepreneurial orientation and culture, innovation, and interdepartmental integration, meaning the collaborative efforts among various departments within an organisation to achieve sustainability goals, were identified (Dicuonzo et al., 2020). Previous authors found that personal values, as well as the desire to give something back to society, are major drivers. Other authors pointed out that ecopreneurs are driven by their green values, seeking to spread these values while also identifying market opportunities for eco-friendly products and services. While monetary motivations are present, they are more about earning a living than profit-driven goals. Passion for their business and its offerings is closely tied to their green values. Further internal motivations of entrepreneurs include ecological and economic values. Ecological values are driven by the desire to reduce pollution and fight climate change. Economic values motivate ecological entrepreneurs through potential cost savings, long-term profits, and government incentives (Robert Isaak, 2016a).

As external drivers for sustainable business practices, the growing consumer awareness and attention to environmental issues, regulations and competitiveness in the market were identified (Dicuonzo et al., 2020). Also, the influence of society, brand reputation, stakeholder pressure as well as increased market pressure can externally influence the starting of a sustainable business. Market pressure is major because customers have significant power to influence a company's performance through their buying choices or by boycotting products (Dhir et al., 2023)

Not only society but also family, which can be considered as society at its smallest scale, is influencing ecopreneurs' motivations as they care about their families and friends' opinions and thoughts (Gunawan et al.,

2021). Individuals who are deeply concerned about their families tend to care about the health of their family members, as well as the well-being of society and the environment for future generations. The stronger the influence of family on a person's values, the more likely it is that their firm will engage in eco-friendly activities. Therefore, valuing family opinions and caring for family health motivate entrepreneurs to adopt sustainable practices. The culture, ethnicity, and religion of entrepreneurs also play important roles in the adoption of ecopreneurship practices, as they shape ethical values and business practices (Hechavarría, 2016).

The literature has also identified other ways to look at the motivators beyond internal and external motivations. Some authors found out that entrepreneurial intentions in sustainable entrepreneurship can follow two paths: one enabled by a supportive environment focusing on sustainability and value creation and another generated as a response to an unsupportive environment. The first path is defined by a strong orientation towards sustainability, the presence of sustainability-focused entrepreneurial ideas, an emphasis on value creation, and the perception of business and social support. In contrast, the second path is marked by a high level of entrepreneurial intention towards sustainability but lacks sustainability-oriented ideas and does not perceive social or contextual support.

Further, Gast et al. (2017) worked out three different categories for the drivers of starting sustainable enterprises—micro-level drivers, meso-level drivers, and macro-level drivers. For micro-level drivers, the authors found that family affects the environmental awareness and the engagement of entrepreneurs, primarily women. Meso-level drivers are external influences of other market players, and macro-level drivers mainly need to comply with regulatory frameworks by governmental or non-governmental institutions, as well as the demands of stakeholders.

5.3.1 Drivers to Implement Circular Economy

As the literature on drivers for sustainable businesses, the literature on factors of implementing the circular economy also mostly distinguishes between internal and external factors.

Internal drivers, primarily revolve around the potential gains associated with product development and increased efficiency in material and energy usage. By transitioning towards a circular model, companies stand to improve the quality of their products, thereby enhancing their market competitiveness and operational efficiency. Additionally, the integration of circular economy principles can attract environmentally conscious consumers, fostering brand loyalty and reinforcing product quality. The authors also mention that internal drivers include the alignment of business principles with circular economy principles, the enthusiasm of managers to expand their understanding of circular economy, and the presence of innovation and technology (Agyemang et al., 2019). The availability of technology and the continuous improvement of it also benefit the implementation of circular business practices.

Externally, the adoption of the circular economy is influenced by a range of factors, as noted by various scholars (Vuorio et al., 2018). Government regulations play a pivotal role in shaping the regulatory framework within which businesses operate, impacting their incentives to adopt sustainable practices (Agyemang et al., 2019). Furthermore, international competition drives companies to innovate and differentiate themselves through sustainable practices, aligning with global environmental standards. De Mattos and De Albuquerque (2018) emphasised the significance of governmental support and geographical proximity as external factors that can facilitate or hinder the implementation of circular economy initiatives. Broader societal and environmental concerns also serve as external drivers for circular economy adoption. Issues such as climate change and reduced environmental impact underscore the urgent need for businesses to mitigate their ecological footprint. Networks are influencing the decision to start green, and consumer awareness and demand for sustainable products put pressure on companies to embrace circular practices, contributing to a shift towards more environmentally responsible production and consumption patterns (Santos-Corrada et al., 2024). Not only does consumer awareness put pressure on companies to change, but external stakeholder changes their priorities.

5.3.2 Drivers to Launch a Born-sustainable Firm

While born sustainable business models play a significant role in the development and enhancement of the circular economy, there remains a lack of theoretical and empirical understanding regarding the factors that drive companies to integrate circular practices in born sustainable firms, particularly within the fashion industry. Therefore, Ostermann et al. (2021) conducted research on the drivers to implement the circular economy in born-sustainable business, using a case study from the fashion industry. They found that internal drivers are more prominent compared to external drivers. The internal drivers elaborated were market strategies, business principles, the commitment of management and staff, know-how, productive process product and service, and innovation. The only external drivers identified were laws and regulations. Dicuonzo et al. (2020) made a multi-case analysis on the key drivers of born-sustainable businesses in the Italian Fashion Industry and their results stated that the culture of the entrepreneur and especially the sensitivity towards environmental issues, play a crucial role in the creation of a green business. Additionally, the entrepreneur's orientation as well as innovation are the main internal factors that motivate born-sustainable businesses. Regarding external factors, Dicuonzo et al. (2020) found that different than in other literature, the latest legislation and the competitiveness in the market do not have an impact on the choice to start a sustainable business, but the growing customer attention to sustainable issues has a great impact. Going even one step further, multiple studies have dealt specifically with the motivation of female entrepreneurs and highlight that they often have multifaceted motivations for engaging in sustainable business practices. Some authors looked at motivations for sustainable business practices and argued that women entrepreneurs are often motivated by a strong sense of social and environmental responsibility. Their motivations go beyond profit to incorporate broader societal and environmental well-being. The identified intrinsic motivations included empathy, selfless gain, and core values. The passions, motivations, and driving forces of these women entrepreneurs were intrinsic to their own unique thought processes, emotions, and decision-making approaches (Cuya-Velásquez et al., 2023).

5.4 Exploring the Challenges of Female Entrepreneurs Engaged in Sustainability

The challenges created by environmental issues in relation to corporate activity refocused the business model of the companies towards a new logic of value creation (Fischer et al., 2018). Entrepreneurship has been recognised as a possible solution to major social and environmental issues like climate change. The emerging field of sustainable and circular entrepreneurship is a powerful factor in the creation of innovative and desirable value for humankind and the earth (Zucchella & Urban, 2019). Following a waste minimisation practice and improving the quality of life (Dean & McMullen, 2007), female entrepreneurs paid particular attention to sustainability (Criado-Gomis et al., 2020). Female entrepreneurs address environmental entrepreneurial goals as they have entrepreneurial intentions in sustainable entrepreneurship (Vuorio et al., 2018).

Female sustainable entrepreneurs may face financial challenges as they need to compete with concurrent who focus on reducing raw material costs and maximising profits through high-volume productions (Criado-Gomis et al., 2020). For these entrepreneurs, "Creating a circular business model may be a first step to dissolving previous alliances. In some cases, this transformation requires companies to improve material selection and switch their current supply of inputs to nontoxic, pure, raw materials." According to (Lahti et al., 2018, p. 3)

Additionally, these entrepreneurs may encounter difficulties in attracting investors who share similar sustainable goals and are aware of the company's market potential (Koirala, 2019). In that case, female sustainable entrepreneurs may rely on technology and crowdfunding platforms as an important source of primary funding and a tool to test the value proposition of the business idea (Ughetto et al., 2020). Their sustainable model may entice investors and citizens ready to commit little sums to support an idea in the circular economy field. Undertaking entrepreneurial activities in circular entrepreneurship requires collaborations and partnerships with several stakeholders to be able to close the loop in the circular economy (Evans et al., 2017). These business ties include suppliers and organisations along the value chain and even with end consumers, as they are considered essential and active participants in the sustainable entrepreneurial ecosystem.

5.5 CASE STUDY OF A SUSTAINABLE FEMALE ENTREPRENEUR IN THE FASHION INDUSTRY

A number of female sustainable firms tell the story of their founders and their beginnings to provide invaluable insights about how to embrace sustainability for their firms. A good example is COEGA.

'Established in 2004, COÉGA Sunwear was launched with the introduction of COÉGA Pool Shoes when I noticed a need for heat resistant & anti-slip safety around pools in & around Dubai as well as fashionable, sun-protective garments for my entire family.

Loving to sew, I took it upon myself to create swimwear for my children & me. COÉGA started with distribution to a single retail outlet in Dubai. What began with a unique pool shoe design has grown into a range of protective & modest swimwear for the whole family.

Today, COÉGA stands as a highly-commended company in the fashion sector, collaborating with major international brands, such as Disney, Marvel, and Warner Bros (Batman, Superman, Looney Tunes, etc.), amongst others.' Source: Coega Website.

The founder was selected in October 2023 as the aspiring Women of the Week by the Womenpreneur Middle East: the magazine published 'A Voyage of Inclusivity and sustainable swimwear 'Maureen Hall represents a beacon of entrepreneurial excellence in the UAE, having founded and led COÉGA Sunwear to its well-deserved reputation as a top-tier swimwear brand. The journey that began in 2004 has evolved into an inspiring tale of determination, innovation, and commitment to inclusivity. Source:www.Womenpreneur.com

---

What Makes COÉGA so Special?
Inclusive Brand
   COÉGA takes pride in its unwavering commitment to inclusivity and modesty. Our diverse swimwear collection embraces all body types and preferences, ensuring that everyone feels comfortable and confident in our designs
   Giving Back
   COÉGA donates 1% of its online sales towards the 'Clean Ocean Initiative'. Over the years, COÉGA has contributed to charitable campaigns like 'Drop Your Shorts For Good,' donating swimwear, the 'PINK-TOBER' campaign, donating proceeds to support Breast Cancer Awareness, and "Stop & Help", providing aid to needy families in 2020.
   Locally Made
   COÉGA Sunwear is proudly home-grown in the UAE. All design, manufacturing & distribution is based in our world headquarters in Jebel Ali, Dubai. Manufacturing in Dubai allows for short lead times and flexible logistics, owing to our strategic geographic location between the Middle East, Asia, Africa & Europe.
   COÉGA Swimwear's Sustainability Practices
   For the company, the term 'sustainability is not a choice. It is a basic need. The founder tries to implement several sustainable practices in her company.

(continued)

(continued)

Materials

We are dedicated to incorporating more recycled and regenerated fabric in our swimwear, with a focus on ECONYL® yarn. This 100% regenerated nylon is made from discarded materials like fishing nets, reducing environmental pollution.

Minimum Waste

We strive towards minimal waste in our production, starting from the initial stage of cutting patterns up to the final stitching. Where possible, we utilise some leftover unused fabric from production to make additional pool shoes.

Packaging

We are aiming to minimise the unnecessary use of packaging material, plastic packaging particularly. Our Hang Tags and Header cards are made out of recyclable materials.

CSR

As part of our social responsibility to give back to the community, we donate 1% of our online sales towards the 'Clean Ocean Initiative'. In the past, we have also supported initiatives like "Drop Your Shorts For Good", "PINK November" and "Stop & Help" providing aid to worthy causes.

Save the Ocean

To reduce impact, we recommend using Cora Ball or Guppy Bag when washing swimwear (even sustainable ones) to prevent microplastic fiber shedding. We sponsored Mangrove planting event with Azraq, who is actively participating. Mangroves protect coastlines, species, livelihoods and combat climate change as carbon-rich forests.

Slow Fashion & Small Batch Production

Our ethos is to encourage slow fashion, supporting sustainable practices. We try to produce in small batches or as per customer orders. Our swimwear is crafted with Lycra XtraLife fabric, ensuring long-lasting comfort, fit and shape, embodying our commitment to reduce landfill waste."

Source: Coega.com website

According to a previous interview with Maureen Hall on FemaleFusion by Manual Jen Blendos (3 July 2024), Maureen's extensive experience as an entrepreneur provides new insight into how to adjust to the constantly changing marketing environment. Her strategy challenges the idea that having many followers is the key performance indicator by highlighting the value of engagement and authenticity in influencer partnerships. Maureen shows how businesses can remain relevant by promoting constant experimentation with marketing strategies in light of the quickly evolving social media landscape. Her advice on producing instructive short-form content sheds light on the shift in marketing towards value-driven strategies that appeal to contemporary consumers. Maureen's fusion of cutting-edge digital strategies with conventional in-store marketing demonstrates a holistic approach to brand building, showing that flexibility and a readiness to try new things are essential for long-term success in today's fast-paced business world.

The story of COEGA is a nice case and a lesson on how female sustainable entrepreneurs shape opportunities. Particularly, it shows how motivated and open-minded female founders can turn a problem, 'Sunburn and sun reaction of the skin,' into an opportunity for business. The story of COEGA Swimwear also illustrates how the foundation of a sustainable firm frequently rests on an entrepreneurial founder team and partners: it is necessary to combine different skills and backgrounds and different points of view to ensure a better design and evaluation of the new business and to run it successfully. Moreover, the story of the company illustrates how the female founder shows a combination of prosocial (Omoto & Snyder, 2010) and intrinsic motivation, an 'inclusive brand' to undertake sustainable entrepreneurial activities to contribute to a better planet and a better world. She expresses professional and ethical traits and has decided to implement sustainable practices and circular business models in her company to adhere to the United Nations' sustainable goals agenda. She is driven by the desire to contribute to the creation of environmental value for the environment and the planet. She paid high attention to using sustainable materials and natural fabric when producing to save the ocean. She also followed a waste minimisation practice.

Another pertinent example of a female who does not run a sustainable firm but actively supports the development of a circular economy through non-profit organisations is represented by a female transformational leader rather than operating a circular business (Zucchella & Urban, 2019). One person who is very significant is Dame Ellen McArthur.

A network of collaborations with businesses, academic institutions, and other organisations has grown around her Foundation, and several projects are in the works. The Global Commitment to End Plastic Waste and Pollution at the Source, which has been signed by 250 organisations—including many of the biggest packaging manufacturers, brands, retailers, recyclers, governments, and non-governmental organisations—is an example of a recent initiative by her Foundation. The Ellen MacArthur Foundation is spearheading the New Plastics Economy Global Commitment in partnership with UN Environment.

Ellen McArthur serves as an example of how being a female sustainable entrepreneur can involve more than just managing a business or undertaking entrepreneurial activities; she has established a think tank specifically to promote the development of the circular economy and organised a large-scale campaign to remove plastic from the ocean.

> **Ellen MacArthur**
> "Dame Ellen MacArthur first hit the headlines in 2001 when she raced single-handedly non-stop around the world in the Vendée Globe when only 24 years old. After 94 days at sea, Ellen returned to a different life. She had come second in one of the hardest races in offshore sailing, and the response was massive. Prior to her Vendée success, she won the solo transatlantic race from the UK to the USA and went on to win the Route du Rhum from France to the Caribbean in 2002. After this successful run in the monohull Open 60 class, Ellen turned her attention to the multihull circuit leading to her departure from Falmouth, UK, in 2004 on board the 75ft trimaran B&Q… she returned 71 days, 14 hours, 18 minutes, 33 seconds later, having sailed over 26,000 miles to become the fastest person to circumnavigate the globe single-handed. She was knighted by the Queen in 2005 and has received the Legion d'Honneur from French President, Nicolas Sarkozy. She is a founder of the Ellen MacArthur Cancer Trust, a charity, set up in 2003, which works with hospitals across the UK to take young people aged between 8–24 sailing, helping them regain their confidence after treatment for cancer & leukemia. Ellen's current and unexpected direction was a

(continued)

(continued)
result of her competitions at sea, which gave her a very real understanding of what it means to rely on a finite supply of resources, as on the boat food, water and fuel were inescapably linked to success or failure. Five years ago this inspired a new journey, spending time with local and national governments, scientists and working across key industry sectors to understand how on land too we rely on finite resources in the form of materials, energy and water. It was through this realisation that Ellen made the difficult decision to end her professional racing career and focus on a still greater challenge. Ellen's search for solutions to these challenges led her to discover a framework for redesign and the idea of shifting from our ultimately limited linear to economy to one that is regenerative by nature. In September 2010 she launched the Ellen MacArthur Foundation with the goal of "accelerating the transition to a regenerative, circular economy". The Foundation works in the three areas of business, education and communication. Not surprisingly—this is the most exciting project that Ellen has worked on to date, and, like with her sailing she is totally immersed in it!"

Source: EllenMacArthur.com website

References

Agyemang, M., Kusi-Sarpong, S., Khan, S. A., Mani, V., Rehman, S. T., & Kusi-Sarpong, H. (2019). Drivers and barriers to circular economy implementation: An explorative study in Pakistan's automobile industry. *Management Decision, 57*(4), 971–994.

Amabile, T. M. (1997). Entrepreneurial creativity through motivational synergy. *The Journal of Creative Behavior, 31*(1), 18–26.

Ambepitiya, K. R. (2016). The role of women entrepreneurs in establishing sustainable development in developing nations. *World Review of Business Research, 6*(1), 161–178.

Apetrei, C. I., Caniglia, G., von Wehrden, H., & Lang, D. J. (2021). Just another buzzword? A systematic literature review of knowledge-related concepts in sustainability science. *Global Environmental Change, 68*, 102222.

Ardichvili, A., Cardozo, R., & Ray, S. (2003). A theory of entrepreneurial opportunity identification and development. *Journal of Business Venturing, 18*(1), 105–123.

Barrachina Fernández, M., García-Centeno, M., & Calderón Patier, C. (2021). Women sustainable entrepreneurship: Review and research agenda. *Sustainability, 13*(21), 12047.

Bhattacharjee, S., & Cruz, J. (2015). Economic sustainability of closed loop supply chains: A holistic model for decision and policy analysis. *Decision Support Systems, 77*, 67–86.

Buttner, E. H., & Moore, D. P. (1997). Women's organisational exodus to entrepreneurship: Self-reported motivations and correlates with success. *Journal of Small Business Management, 35*, 34–46.

Capra, F., & Mattei, U. (2015). *The ecology of law: Toward a legal system in tune with nature and community*. Berrett-Koehler Publishers.

Cohen, B., & Winn, M. I. (2007). Market imperfections, opportunity and sustainable entrepreneurship. *Journal of Business Venturing, 22*(1), 29–49.

Colombelli, A., D'Ambrosio, A., & Ravetti, C. (2024). Women in innovative start-ups and regional inclusiveness: 'Green'and socially-responsible companies. *Regional Studies*, 1–14.

Criado-Gomis, A., Iniesta-Bonillo, M.-A., Cervera-Taulet, A., & Ribeiro-Soriano, D. (2020). Women as key agents in sustainable entrepreneurship: A gender multigroup analysis of the SEO-performance relationship. *Sustainability, 12*(3), 1244.

Cullen, U. A., & De Angelis, R. (2021). Circular entrepreneurship: A business model perspective. *Resources, Conservation and Recycling, 168*, 105300.

Cuya-Velásquez, B. B., Alvarez-Risco, A., de las Mercedes Anderson-Seminario, M., & Del-Aguila-Arcentales, S. (2023). Creation of sustainable enterprises from the female directionality. In *Footprint and entrepreneurship: Global green initiatives* (pp. 163–187). Springer.

De Mattos, C. A., & De Albuquerque, T. L. M. (2018). Enabling factors and strategies for the transition toward a circular economy (CE). *Sustainability, 10*(12), 4628.

de Oliveira, C. T., & Oliveira, G. G. A. (2023). What circular economy indicators really measure? An overview of circular economy principles and sustainable development goals. *Resources, Conservation and Recycling, 190*, 106850.

Dean, T. J., & McMullen, J. S. (2007). Toward a theory of sustainable entrepreneurship: Reducing environmental degradation through entrepreneurial action. *Journal of Business Venturing, 22*(1), 50–76.

Debnath, G. C., Chowdhury, S., Khan, S., Farahdina, T., & Chowdhury, T. S. (2019). Role of women entrepreneurship on achieving sustainable development goals (SDGs) in Bangladesh. *The Business & Management Review, 10*(5), 130–140.

Dhir, A., Khan, S. J., Islam, N., Ractham, P., & Meenakshi, N. (2023). Drivers of sustainable business model innovations. An upper echelon theory perspective. *Technological Forecasting and Social Change, 191*, 122409.

Dicuonzo, G., Galeone, G., Ranaldo, S., & Turco, M. (2020). The key drivers of born-sustainable businesses: Evidence from the Italian fashion industry. *Sustainability, 12*(24), 10237.

Evans, S., Vladimirova, D., Holgado, M., Van Fossen, K., Yang, M. Y., Silva, E. A., & Barlow, C. Y. (2017). Business model innovation for sustainability: Towards a unified perspective for creation of sustainable business models. *Business Strategy and the Environment, 26*(5), 597–608.

European Commission. (2018). Circular economy—Implementation of the Circular Economy Action Plan. http://ec.europa.eu/environment/circular-economy/index_en.htm. Accessed January 17, 2018.

Fischer, D., Mauer, R., & Brettel, M. (2018). Regulatory focus theory and sustainable entrepreneurship. *International Journal of Entrepreneurial Behavior & Research, 24*(2), 408–428.

Galvão, G. D. A., Homrich, A. S., Geissdoerfer, M., Evans, S., Scoleze Ferrer, P. S., & Carvalho, M. M. (2020). Towards a value stream perspective of circular business models. *Resources, Conservation and Recycling, 162*, 105060.

Gast, J., Gundolf, K., & Cesinger, B. (2017). Doing business in a green way: A systematic review of the ecological sustainability entrepreneurship literature and future research directions. *Journal of Cleaner Production, 147*, 44–56.

Gauthier, C., & Gilomen, B. (2016). Business models for sustainability: Energy efficiency in urban districts. *Organisation & Environment, 29*(1), 124–144.

Gibbs, D. (2006). Sustainability entrepreneurs, ecopreneurs and the development of a sustainable economy. *Greener Management International, 55*, 63–78.

Greco, A., & de Jong, G. (2017). Sustainable entrepreneurship: Definitions, themes and research gaps. *Centre for Sustainable Entrepreneurship, Working paper 1706*.

Guan, N. H., Ahmad, N. H., Rahman, S. A., & Halim, H. A. (2020). Towards a sustainable agenda: Enhancing green entrepreneurship image among manufacturing SMEs. *World Review of Entrepreneurship, Management and Sustainable Development, 16*(5), 466–491.

Gunawan, A. A., van Riel, A. A., & Essers, C. (2021). What drives ecopreneurship in women and men? A structured literature review. *Journal of Cleaner Production, 280*, 124336.

Hechavarría, D. M. (2016). Mother nature's son? The impact of gender socialisation and culture on environmental venturing. *International Journal of Gender and Entrepreneurship, 8*(2), 137–172.

Isaak, R. (2016a). Ecopreneurship, rent-seeking, and free-riding in global context: Job-creation without ecocide. *Small Enterprise Research, 23*(1), 85–93.

Isaak, R. (2016b). The making of the ecopreneur. In *Making Ecopreneurs* (pp. 63–78). Routledge.

Kabbara, D., Qin, E., Jarrar, H., & Salloum, C. (2024). Internationalisation and growth of small sustainable fashion enterprises. *International Journal of Entrepreneurship and Small Business, 51*(4), 469–493.

Koirala, S. (2019). SMEs: Key drivers of green and inclusive growth.

Kuckertz, A., & Wagner, M. (2010). The influence of sustainability orientation on entrepreneurial intentions—Investigating the role of business experience. *Journal of Business Venturing, 25*(5), 524–539.

Lacy, P., & Rutqvist, J. (2016). *Waste to wealth: The circular economy advantage*. Springer.

Lahti, T., Wincent, J., & Parida, V. (2018). A definition and theoretical review of the circular economy, value creation, and sustainable business models: Where are we now and where should research move in the future? *Sustainability, 10*(8), 2799.

Lüdeke-Freund, F., Froese, T., Dembek, K., Rosati, F., & Massa, L. (2024). What makes a business model sustainable? Activities, design themes, and value functions. *Organisation & Environment*.

MacArthur, E. (2013). Towards the circular economy. *Journal of Industrial Ecology, 2*, 23–44.

Muo, I., Oladimeji, M., & Agboola, O. (2023). Women entrepreneurship and sustainable development goals (SDGS) in Nigeria. *Fuoye Journal of Management, Innovation and Entrepreneurship, 2*(2).

Omoto, A. M., & Snyder, M. (2010). Influences of psychological sense of community on voluntary helping and prosocial action. In *The psychology of prosocial behavior: Group processes, intergroup relations, and helping* (pp. 223–244). Wiley.

Ostermann, C. M., Nascimento, L., Steinbruch, F. K., & Callegaro-de-Menezes, D. (2021). Drivers to implement the circular economy in born-sustainable business models: A case study in the fashion industry. *Revista de Gestão, 28*(3), 223–240.

Outsios, G., & Farooqi, S. A. (2017). Gender in sustainable entrepreneurship: Evidence from the UK. *Gender in Management: An International Journal*.

Paolone, F., Pozzoli, M., Chhabra, M., & Di Vaio, A. (2024). Cultural and gender diversity for ESG performance towards knowledge sharing: Empirical evidence from European banks. *Journal of Knowledge Management, 28*(11), 106–131.

Pearce, D. W., & Turner, R. K. (1989). *Economics of natural resources and the environment*. Johns Hopkins University Press.

Santos-Corrada, M. D. L. M., Méndez-Tejeda, R., Flecha-Ortiz, J. A., & Lopez, E. (2024). An analysis of sustainable consumption practices through the role of the consumer behavior in the circular economy. *Journal of Consumer Behaviour, 23*(1), 229–242.

Tilley, F., & Parrish, B. D. (2006). From poles to wholes: Facilitating an integrated approach to sustainable entrepreneurship. *World Review of Entrepreneurship, Management and Sustainable Development, 2*(4), 281–294.

Ughetto, E., Rossi, M., Audretsch, D., & Lehmann, E. E. (2020). Female entrepreneurship in the digital era. *Small Business Economics, 55*(2), 305–312.

Vuorio, A. M., Puumalainen, K., & Fellnhofer, K. (2018). Drivers of entrepreneurial intentions in sustainable entrepreneurship. *International Journal of Entrepreneurial Behavior & Research.*

Zucchella, A., & Urban, S. (2014). Futures of the sustainable firm: An evolutionary perspective. *Futures, 63*, 86–100.

Zucchella, A., & Urban, S. (2019). *Circular entrepreneurship.* Springer.

CHAPTER 6

Social Transformative Entrepreneurship: The Emergence of Female Migrant Entrepreneurs

Abstract Entrepreneurship can best position its potential of inclusivity and transformativity in the case of female migrants. Many women, in their pursuit of economic and social legitimation, migrate and embark on entrepreneurial journeys to escape the scarcity of opportunities. This facet of entrepreneurship studies promises to enrich the content and extend the boundaries of the discipline. This chapter will discuss the main typologies of entrepreneurship as linked to migration flows, the opportunities that arise from migration, the challenges female migrant entrepreneurs face, and their motivation to undertake entrepreneurial activities in the host country. The chapter concludes with a case study about 'Yorkshire Damacheese', a case of a successful Syrian migrant entrepreneur in the food industry.

Keywords Migrant entrepreneurship • Migration • Social transformation • Liabilities • Opportunities • Female migrant entrepreneur

© The Author(s), under exclusive license to Springer Nature Switzerland AG 2025
D. Kabbara, *Transformative Entrepreneurship in the Global Landscape*, https://doi.org/10.1007/978-3-031-77141-5_6

6.1 Exploring International Entrepreneurship Typologies Associated with Migration

An important and growing stream in entrepreneurship is linked to migration flows. Though public opinion sometimes views migrants as a threat to their living standards and domestic culture, they can develop in the destination countries innovations (Lissoni, 2018, p. 108) and entrepreneurship (Kerr & Kerr, 2020), bridging communities, countries, and cultures. (Parrilli et al., 2019) coined the term "communities-on-move," playing an important role in the entrepreneurial activity of their members and described as cultural communities marked by their own social capital, that is, shared values and network ties, which provide tacit knowledge and opportunities to their members and facilitate their integration in their host regions and countries" (ibid,. p. 1). According to the International Organisation for Migration (IOM), migration fosters interaction between migrants as individuals and communities of origin, transit, and destination. As such, it catalyses social change and development at both macro and micro levels. Societies thus transform their social structures, identities, attitudes, norms, and practices. Transnationalism, the process by which individuals create and preserve socio-cultural ties and political borders, is a common phenomenon when mobility patterns are growing more complex, and almost every nation is subject to migration in some capacity. As a result, many countries are looking for practical ways to deal with the social changes brought about by human mobility in the twenty-first century. IOM wants to present migration as one of the answers to the world's problems, like helping communities thrive economically or adjusting to the effects of climate change.

The mentioned phenomena of migrations have been accompanied by a surge in academic research about entrepreneurship forms related to these flows. These studies have witnessed the convergence of different theoretical perspectives, from entrepreneurship and international entrepreneurship to International Business. They have also witnessed a wealth of studies of alternative forms of entrepreneurship arising from migrations. Concepts like immigrant (Rath & Kloosterman, 2000), ethnic (Zhou, 2004), diaspora (Cohen, 2008), and transnational and refugee entrepreneurship (Fong et al., 2007) have been developed. Though they share several commonalities, the main one being their relatedness to the migration flows, they also show some distinctive features. The latter illustrates that these entrepreneurs have both overlaps and differences. International entrepreneurs, transnational entrepreneurs and diaspora entrepreneurs are entrepreneurs who branch out from the domestic market to pursue a competitive advantage (Drori et al., 2009; Elo et al., 2018). However, differences can be noted from several perspectives. First, concerning the type of entrepreneur, the international entrepreneur is an internationally oriented individual (McDougall & Oviatt, 2000; Oviatt & McDougall, 2005), while transnational entrepreneurs, diaspora entrepreneurs, Ethnic entrepreneurs and refugee entrepreneurs are all immigrant individuals (Chen & Tan, 2009; Shepherd et al., 2019) and share distinctive language and custom. Second, with regard to the entrepreneur's embeddedness, international entrepreneurs are embedded in an international environment. Transnational entrepreneurs and diasporas entrepreneurs leverage opportunities that arise from their mixed embeddedness in dual social fields' bifocality (Kloosterman et al., 1998), and in two geographical locations (Home and host country) (Cohen, 2008; Drori et al., 2006). Ethnic entrepreneurs and refugee entrepreneurs are embedded in one country. They focus on their entrepreneurial activities within the host country (Fong et al., 2007; Lindley, 2009; Waldinger et al., 1990). In particular, ethnic entrepreneurs leverage opportunities that ascend from their group's ethnic sources and social capital in the host country (Drori et al., 2009; Zhou, 2004). In terms of the entrepreneur's motivation to be an entrepreneur in the host country, international entrepreneurs, transnational entrepreneurs, and diaspora entrepreneurs experience a 'pull' motivation to entrepreneurial activities in the host country as they discover opportunities outside the domestic markets (Chen & Tan, 2009; Oviatt & McDougall, 1997; Zahra & George, 2002). Ethnic entrepreneurs and Refugee entrepreneurs experience a 'push' motivation or a necessity to be engaged in entrepreneurial activity in the host country (Fong et al., 2007; Yinger, 1994). They frequently enter self-employment due to the disadvantages they face as immigrants in the host country's labour market (Phizacklea & Ram, 1996). In particular, refugee entrepreneurs are forced to establish a business in the host country because they cannot retain any linkage or business relations with their native or home country because of serious events or threats in their home country (Fong et al., 2007; Wauters & Lambrecht, 2008).

Streams about ethnic entrepreneurship (Zhou, 2004), immigrant entrepreneurship (Zolin & Schlosser, 2013), and refugee entrepreneurship (Wauters & Lambrecht, 2008) do not necessarily leverage transnational linkages. They may target a local market in the host country and/or the bi-directional links between the origin and the host country. The links with the country of origin may relate to the supply of goods and services (Zhou, 2004). International Entrepreneurship does not specifically address the case of immigrants' entrepreneurial activity, but its broad definition can encompass it, particularly when it involves the exploration and exploitation of opportunities across borders. There is a call for more studies about the topic, especially in its positioning in IE: "We start challenging the basis of what constitutes the international and the entrepreneur in international entrepreneurship (IE) by relating international entrepreneurship to migration, migrants and diasporas, and their transnational and international ventures as dimensions rarely studied." (Elo et al., 2018, p. 119).

Additionally, there is a call for more studies for further contextualisation in research on immigrants, particularly to highlight the complex contextual setting of migrants and relate it to the arena of their focal activity (Zahra et al., 2014). Furthermore, it is noted that several research studies have frequently focused on immigrant men as entrepreneurs, and female immigrant entrepreneurship has been studied less (Collins & Low, 2010; Marchand et al., 2014).

Migrant entrepreneurship literature characterises how migrant actors frequently live out their lives across borders as they cultivate multi-layered and multisided identifications in and across local, regional, and national spaces. These varied spaces consist of "differing forms, depth, and breadth" as "a set of multiple interlocking networks of social relationships through which ideas, practices, and resources are unequally exchanged, organised, and transformed" (Levitt & Schiller, 2004, p. 1009). Migrant entrepreneurs are defined as individuals who migrate from one country to another while simultaneously maintaining business linkages to home and host cultures. Table 6.1 summarises the key characteristics of these domains and compares them. Migrant entrepreneurship in the context of international entrepreneurship: immigration entrepreneurship is a subset of international entrepreneurship that merits special attention. Immigrant entrepreneurs who establish firms in new countries contribute not only to their own integration but also to the economic growth and transformation of their host nations. Despite the specific challenges immigrant entrepreneurs face, such as linguistic and cultural barriers, their businesses have a significant positive economic impact, both locally and internationally. For instance, their unique perspectives and experiences enrich the entrepreneurial ecosystem, fostering diversity, innovation, and cross-cultural

Table 6.1 Different entrepreneurship streams related to migration

Field	Definition	Type of entrepreneurs	Key features	Dominant locus
Immigrant entrepreneurship	Undertaking entrepreneurial activities, in particular creating new businesses by first- or second-generation immigrants	Immigrant entrepreneurs are 'individuals who move into a country for a permanent settlement.'	• Immigrant entrepreneurs • Response to 'Push' or 'Pull' factors for entrepreneurship in the host country • Entrepreneurs' embeddedness in the host country	• Host country
Transnational entrepreneurship	Transnational entrepreneurs (TEs) are individuals who migrate from one country to another, concurrently maintaining business-related linkages between their former country of origin and the currently adopted countries and communities.	Transnational entrepreneurs are 'migrants engaged in two or more socially embedded environments, maintaining global relations enhancing creativity and maximising their resource base.'	• Migrant entrepreneurs • Entrepreneur's embeddedness in a dual environment • Voluntary nature of the move: response to 'Pull' factors to entrepreneurship	• country • Host country
Ethnic entrepreneurship	The study of entrepreneurial activity based on connections and interactions between people who have common origins and share migration experiences	Ethnic entrepreneurs are 'immigrants often with distinctive language and customs; engaged in formal, informal, or illegal self-employment and/or businesses in the adopted country.'	• Immigrant entrepreneurs • Entrepreneur's embeddedness in the host country • Response to the 'Push' factor to entrepreneurship in host country • Rely on the group's ethnic resources • Group membership is tied to a common cultural heritage and is known to out-of-group members as having such a trait	• Host country

(continued)

Table 6.1 (continued)

Field	Definition	Type of entrepreneurs	Key features	Dominant locus
Diaspora entrepreneurship	Diaspora entrepreneurship is not limited to the first generation of ethnic and migrant entrepreneurs but also covers the second and third generations.	Diaspora entrepreneurs are 'Migrants and their descendants who maintain a strong emotional relationship with their country of origin'; they are settled in a country other than their country of origin, plus they have a cultural understanding of both their host and home country.	• Migrant entrepreneurs • Well-connected to their home country • Entrepreneur's embeddedness in a dual environment	• Home country • Host country
Refugee entrepreneurship	Refugee entrepreneurship involves refugees who start businesses and become entrepreneurs in their new home countries.	Refugee entrepreneurs are "those persons who are outside their country of nationality or habitual residence and unable to return there owing to serious and indiscriminate threats to life, physical integrity or freedom resulting from generalised violence or events seriously disturbing public order."	• Immigrant entrepreneurs • Entrepreneur's embeddedness in the host country • 'Push' factor for migration and entrepreneurship because of conflict in the home country	• Host country

Source: Kabbara and Zucchella (2023)

exchange. Corporate entrepreneurship can play a supportive role in this context by providing a platform for immigrant entrepreneurs within established companies, harnessing their unique insights and experiences to drive innovation and explore new market opportunities.

6.2 Leveraging Network for Female Migrant Entrepreneurship

A person's ex-ante entrepreneurial experience is greatly influenced by their social environment. People who live in socially diverse environments are compelled to have a more accepting attitude towards different communities and their customs (Al Sayah et al., 2023). Culture, according to Hong et al. (2000), is the interpretation of a significant amount of knowledge and customs. Knowledge is acquired through a significant amount of years of experience that is passed down from generation to generation and is interpreted by the customs that the relevant group of people adhered to in order to adapt to their social, natural, and living environments. These customs are always changing, indicating that societies' cultural identities change in tandem with their surroundings. The unique experiences of every individual can also be seen as indicators of diversity in societies. The significance of female entrepreneurs' networks in their entrepreneurial pursuits has been highlighted by extant research on female (migrant) entrepreneurship (McAdam et al., 2019). Building on their cultural and religious beliefs, female immigrant entrepreneurs have the potential to link the global community centred around a particular industry with a unique consumer culture. Examples of an industry (modest clothing, halal cuisine, etc.) that crosses national boundaries and provides the perfect setting for examining the opportunities and difficulties Muslim women encounter when pursuing entrepreneurship in the host nations. When it comes to theorising about diversity and inclusion in international business, these sectors provide a means of emancipation (Kabbara & Zucchella, 2023).

Networks are the connections an entrepreneur has with other businesses and people in the larger community. In order to obtain information and tangible resources (capital, skills) that are hard to come by in the market or to accelerate their internationalisation process (Zucchella & Kabbara, 2013), female entrepreneurs may depend on personal and professional relationships (Munkejord, 2017). The goals of the female entrepreneur will be attainable with the help of these resources. Numerous kinds of networks were acknowledged as essential in the literature on female entrepreneurship. Many authors have noted the ways in which female entrepreneurs are enabled to engage in entrepreneurial activities by border-spanning networks based on family ties (Mustafa & Chen, 2010), business ties (Munkejord, 2017), community ties (Chrysostome & Lin, 2010), and ethnic ties (Pruthi et al., 2018). According to McAdam et al. (2019), these connections are regarded as social capital and are crucial to the network of female entrepreneurs.

6.2.1 Family Network

One of the most promising research areas in transformative international entrepreneurship is the role of networks and interpersonal relationships in the launch and internationalisation process of entrepreneurial firms (Kabbara, 2009; Zucchella & Kabbara, 2011). The network's value in comprehending the growth and prosperity of global entrepreneurial enterprises has been repeatedly demonstrated. International new ventures must rely on alternate forms of control because they lack the resources to own and control a large number of assets.

Female migrant entrepreneurs acquire valuable resources through the migrant family network ties, and hence, they confirm the hypothesis that family represents an important source of network ties in which entrepreneurs can be embedded in "family embeddedness" (Aldrich & Cliff, 2003). Family ties have distinctive characteristics, resulting in a particular type of social capital. Due to a diaspora and wide migration of the original family and friends(Cohen, 2008; Safran, 1991), these social ties spread across countries and create glocal network (Chen & Tan, 2009). Bonding networks, created through transnational family social ties, provide different types of resources, which are vital to undertaking migrant entrepreneurial activities. For instance, as a female and mother entrepreneur, as mentioned in the previous chapter, managing work and family responsibilities is one of the major challenges women face. Hence, migrant family ties deliver balancing work and family (Brzozowski et al., 2017; Ezzedeen & Zikic, 2017). Additionally, it provides emotional support, which generates emotional stability and psychic resources and helps the transnational female entrepreneur by increasing motivation, commitment, and confidence. In addition to providing these resources, our respondents underlined that migrant family social ties provided a tangible source of capital and ready access to business resources. The latter can be delivered not only as "patient" financial capital, which does not require repayment in the short term, but also as physical capital (equipment) and labour. Moreover, migrant family ties also provided organisational skills and knowledge, allowing them to access business advice characterised by high quality and rapidity at low cost. Therefore, family members, especially partners, help the female migrant entrepreneur set up individual businesses. In this manner, these members could represent a significant proportion of transnational entrepreneurial activity and create a family entrepreneurial team (Discua Cruz et al., 2013)

6.2.2 Community Network

Modern society develops communities around interests and skills more than around locality. Sphered labelled the term community of inquiry defined as "potential stakeholders that provide feedback on the veracity of the potential opportunity" (Shepherd, 2015, p. 491) as a body of contacts that promotes social learning for opportunity development. These potential stakeholders can include potential customers, mentors, investors, and technological experts. Saxton et al. (2016) marked the term Venture advocates as "local venture-community members, as potential stakeholders, that help founders in the developmental stages of emerging enterprises" to be positively related to a new venture's likelihood of launch and survival (Saxton et al., 2016, p. 108). Previous literature has identified two major uses of the term community. The first is the 'territorial and geographical' notion of community—neighbourhood, town, city. The second is "relational," concerned with the "quality of character of human relationship, without reference to location" (Gusfield, 1975, p. 16). The social and cultural context has a big impact on how female migrant entrepreneurs navigate their complex identities through entrepreneurship. For example, prior studies indicate that women seek freedom from current limits in their cultural, technological, social, and economic contexts through entrepreneurship (Rindova et al., 2009). However, female migrant entrepreneurs can integrate and be embedded into their community.

The community of shared values consists of individuals who carry with them their cultural heritage and share the same values and beliefs that promote trust and cooperation (Parrilli et al., 2019). The community groups provide a common symbol system (e.g., rites of passage, language, dress) as boundaries intentionally to create social distance between members. They are considered a community of inquiry, an informal body of stakeholders with a shared interest in a potential opportunity who will try to attract potential stakeholders. The religious associations and charity associations encompass individuals who share 'the sense of community' (Rovai, 2002). These individuals share a sense of community defined as belonging among members, a feeling that members matter to each other and the group, and a common belief that members' needs will be met by their commitment to being together. The members of this community work to find a way to suit people together so that people meet others' needs while fulfilling their own needs. In addition to providing cultural and spiritual continuity in the host country, the religious associations—embedded in the community on the move—served as a communication hub for economic opportunities. In particular, by participating in several cultural and religious events, female entrepreneurs are able to find avenues for social advancement, community service, and respect. Muslim) and family and friends to explore opportunities.

Migrant communities encompass individuals spread across different regions of the world (1) majority females, who carry the heritage of their story to HC, (2) dispersed worldwide, (3) share the same religion and culture and provide a sense of belonging, (4) share a common industry interest, and (5) are connected through the internet. Transnational communities, also composed of relatives and friends, are considered 'social containers' (Djelic & Quack, 2010, p. 14). Female migrant entrepreneurs relied on their glocal network with the community-based. In particular, they relied on local network' clustering effects' with the migrant communities within the host country and non-local networking activities' networking effect' with the diaspora communities that connect ethnic communities worldwide and with their country of origin. The availability of abundant information from the transnational community through social networks, either in the host country or globally, and through the internet inspires female migrant entrepreneurs and enables them to access the market. These transnational communities create international social capital. Therefore, Female migrant entrepreneurs could explore opportunities and develop entrepreneurship in their destination countries (Kerr & Kerr, 2020).

It is significant to stress the crucial role of technology, linking dispersed communities, families, and business actors across countries and enhancing global social and business ties. Technology helps connect a dispersed community and nurtures social ties; it also serves as an exchange of ideas and consumer insights, supports opportunities formation, and enables early product testing and receiving feedback. It also supports the business ecosystem because the latter is highly dispersed. Competencies and resources are owned by different players in various locations.

6.3 Challenges for Female Migrant Entrepreneurs

Female migrant entrepreneurs from ethnic minorities may need to overcome additional contextual constraints (other female entrepreneurs) in the host country. The 'double disadvantage' of gender and ethnicity (De Vita et al., 2014) may increase financial institutions' distrust of migrant women's entrepreneurial ability and force them to rely more on family support to tackle these constraints. Female migrant entrepreneurs may face challenges because of prejudice against their socio-cultural background, leading to lower acceptance in the host country. These biases may contribute to a "feeling of inferiority" (Gonzalez-Gonzalez et al., 2011, p. 368). Previous literature on female entrepreneurship has stressed the challenges female entrepreneurs face in accessing information, networks (Poggesi et al., 2016) and capital (Brush et al., 2009). The 'double disadvantage' of gender and ethnicity of female migrant entrepreneurs may increase financial institutions' distrust and limit their financial capital. Women's self-restraints stem from the fact that women are subjected to cultural barriers that uphold the traditional division of labour and establish a two-tiered system due to the "persistent gendering of entrepreneurship through language and stereotypes embedded in entrepreneurial contexts."

According to their religious background, some authors have written about the dual stigmas that migrant entrepreneurs face: the religious stigma and the migrant stigma (Moufakkir, 2020). Another layer of stigma is added by being a woman. The vulnerability of female migrant entrepreneurs to prejudice and stigma is significant. Due to their desire to become independent by starting their own business (Kabbara et al., 2025), they are also susceptible to animosity within their own communities. This may be especially true for women in Western nations who are starting their own businesses and come from more marginalised communities. Their business value proposition may be more vulnerable to prejudice and stigma if it is ingrained in both unique consumer culture and cultural values. From this perspective, exemplar industries can be food and fashion.

Female migrant entrepreneurs are subject to "a threefold neglect in terms of research on entrepreneurs: as members of a minority group, as women and as immigrant female entrepreneurs" (De Luca & Ambrosini, 2019). Female migrants encounter various forms of liabilities during their entrepreneurial journey, including the liabilities associated with their foreignness, origin, gender, newness, and smallness.

Notwithstanding their motivations (pull or push)—as addressed in the previous chapter, for starting a business, migrant entrepreneurs frequently encounter greater challenges than native entrepreneurs in adjusting to the formal (such as laws) and informal (such as the manner in which business transactions are conducted) institutions of the host nation, which differ from those in their home country (Suárez-Ortega & García-Cabrera, 2022).

Female migrant women entrepreneurs are affected by the liability of foreignness, especially the risk of discrimination "due to differential treatment meted by the host country laws and consumers (Kogan, 2006)" (Kumar et al., 2022, p. 690). They may face challenges due to prejudice against their socio-cultural backgrounds (Chreim et al., 2018). These biases may contribute to a "feeling of inferiority" (Gonzalez-Gonzalez et al., 2011, p. 368). In addition, they may live in a foreign host culture that is different from their culture of origin and religious background, making them vulnerable to the "double stigma" i.e. migrant and religious stigma. Furthermore, female migrant entrepreneurs may face the liabilities of newness (Barth & Zalkat, 2020) and smallness (Stinchcombe, 1965). Literature refers to these liabilities to the venture, being new/inexperienced and resources-poor, but these attributes can be extended to the founder. Lack of experience and resources can limit the growth potential of the venture and increase the likelihood of failure. Female entrepreneurs are supposed to face more barriers, mainly due to lack of experience and more difficult access to finance (Kalleberg & Leicht, 1991). In addition, they may have fewer abilities and capabilities to start a business than their male counterparts (Arenius & Minniti, 2005).

6.4 Opportunities for Female Migrant Entrepreneurs

Female migrant entrepreneurs may take advantage of their multiple identities (from home and host country) caused by migration and their mixed embeddedness in multiple countries (Solano, 2020) to reduce their marginalisation in the host country and explore entrepreneurial opportunities (Kerr & Kerr, 2020). Female migrant entrepreneurs, drawing on their multilingual knowledge base and multicultural background, can bridge communities, countries, and cultures (Morgan et al., 2021) and contribute to value creation at multiple levels (Kabbara, 2023). They are primarily opportunity developers, and even in highly challenging contexts, they may turn this problem into a competitive advantage for the immigrant, depending on the entrepreneurial context and strategy (Gurău et al., 2020).

Contrary to the stereotype of female migrant entrepreneurs, a small-scale business can achieve much more than self-employment in low-value-added businesses. These women work in a range of industries, including digital services, and are capable of starting businesses and creating jobs with room to grow. They can use their inventiveness, creativity, and innovation as standout aspects of their resourcefulness when working with traditional industries.

By contributing to social value creation, female migrant entrepreneurs could find avenues for social advancement, female leadership, and community service in their host countries. The economic value created was critical in achieving the key motivations of female immigrant entrepreneurs: economic autonomy and job creation, which gave them empowerment and recognition and rewarded their families for the support provided. A successful small-scale business owned by a female immigrant entrepreneur gives women financial independence, social recognition, and, most importantly, personal fulfilment.

6.5 Case Study of a Successful Case of Female Migrant Entrepreneur in the Food Industry

A number of female migrant entrepreneurs tell their story and their beginnings to provide invaluable insights about how to launch new firms in the host country and leverage the culture. A good example is Yorkshire DAMACHEESE, which is 'the Halloumi squeaky cheese in the UK'.

'Razan Alsous' is from Syria; she entered the United Kingdom in 2012, after the war in Italy. She has a passion for food, so she decided to launch a halloumi cheese' typical Syrian cheese, for the first time in the United Kingdom. In 2023, she was shortlisted for the prestigious Great British Entrepreneurs Awards in the Entrepreneur category. The cheese's true quality was highlighted when she won the World Cheese Award Bronze Prize 2014/15 after only four months of production. Al Sous has shared her success with renowned chefs such as James Martin, Nadiya Hussein, and the well-known UK duo, the Hairy Bikers, and her company has won forty awards.

The royal family has also endorsed her. "By the end of 2016, the Princess Royal expressed a strong desire to visit us after learning about our story from the royal office" (Source: Damacheese, website).

> **Yorkshire DAMA CHEESE the Halloumi Squeaky cheese CO.**
> Yorkshire DAMA story
>
> Yorkshire Dama Cheese is a story of inspirational bravery by a woman who refused to let her circumstances define or constrain her. It is about finding a new place to call home and new experiences, which has led to the creation of a British multi-award-winning cheese and dairy company.
>
> The story of the founder Razan AlSous
>
> "We came to the UK after the war in Syria in 2012. With my husband and three young children, we had lost almost everything and had to settle into a new life in Yorkshire.
>
> Initially, I began searching for a job, but despite having a pharmacy degree and a scientific background, my lack of references and work history in the UK made it extremely difficult.
>
> Share brand and product details
>
> I came up with the following:
>
> I have a strong microbiological background, having graduated from the Medical Institute in Syria.
>
> My husband is an electronic engineer who ran his own business supplying the pharmaceutical and food industries in Syria with Quality Control labs.
>
> I was now living in Yorkshire where the wonderful, high-quality milk is available locally (and I believe it is a national value).
>
> The government is very supportive of the creation of start-up businesses.
>
> Nowadays, the Syrian cheese (a squeaky semi-hard cheese) that I know and eat every day for breakfast in Syria is very trendy in the UK, and British people love eating it!
>
> After some time, I started to look at other options. I have three children and wanted so badly to build a bright future for them. So I started to think about what was around me—the expertise I could tap into, the sources of support and other opportunities available to me."

(continued)

> **(continued)**
> YORKSHIRE DAMA CHEESE AWARD WINNING CHEESE
> We're so proud of what we do because we know it's the hard work of every member of our team.
> We're lucky enough to have been recognised recently at the British Cheese Awards, World Cheese Awards, International Cheese Awards, World Cheese Award Gold Prize 2015–16, British Cheese Award Silver 2016 for the plain Halloumi, Best Cheese in Yorkshire 2016 for the Chilli Halloumi, Silver for British Cheese Award 2017 for the mint Halloumi, Shortlisted best cheese in Yorkshire 2016 for the Spreadable yogurt
> Razan was nominated by the Prime Minister for International Womens' Day 2015, Woman of the Year 2016, Silver Royal Highland show 2017, Gold for the spreadable yogurt Great Yorkshire Show 2017, Gold for the British cheese award 2018 for the original flavour, Bronze for the British cheese award for the Rosemary Squeaky cheese 2018, Great test 2018 for the original flavour, Champion for the best-added flavour at Great Yorkshire Show for the Rosemary Squeaky cheese, the Best cheese in Yorkshire Taste Award DY 2018 for the Rosemary Squeaky cheese.
> Source: Yorkshiredamacheese.co website

In our case, Razan was able to cope with her multiple layered identities and transform them into a commitment to entrepreneurial opportunities. She leveraged family ties and community to explore and exploit opportunities across boundaries in the food industry, motivated by prosocial and intrinsic motivation. Dama cheese opportunities stem from the female migrant entrepreneur's embeddedness in a cross-national context. DamaCheese case also underlines the role of culture in the process of migrant entrepreneurship from the opportunity lens.

According to a previous interview with Razan published on CNN by Manual Arthur Kirby (27 June 2017), and on BBC by Oli Constable (17 April, 2024), Razan arrived in the UK in 2012 following her husband's business being destroyed by a bombing brought on by the Syrian conflict.

Seeking a better life for herself and her three children, she travelled to the UK. She moved with her brother and parents as well. Because of the Syrian conflict, she applied for a visa as an "asylum seeker" as soon as she got to the UK. English is one of the three languages she speaks. She had studied microbiology in Syria prior to her migration to the UK, but the war had forced her to stop. She thought her husband would be able to get employment in the United Kingdom. Her goal was to continue her education in the UK. However, as an international migrant student, it was extremely challenging to continue attending the university. As a result, she made the decision to hunt for employment, particularly since they had lost everything in Syria as a result of the country's devastation and inflation. Sadly, no employer would hire her because she was a recent immigrant who had trouble finding work in addition to being a mother of three small children.

After giving it some thought, she started to think about her abilities. The change began when she was in her neighbourhood grocery looking for the typical Syrian-Middle Eastern cheese called "Halloumi" to buy for her kids. She accomplished this by experimenting with the product at home using her knowledge of microbiology. To help her find the correct formula, she had to read recipes written in Arabic. When she attempted to investigate the halloumi market in the UK, she discovered that there is only one factory near London, and it does not supply the whole market. After drafting a business plan, she realised she would need a substantial sum of money to get her venture off the ground. She applied for a bank loan through the program for start-up loans. With this meagre budget, she was able to purchase used kitchenware that wasn't intended for cheesemaking and modify it to make halloumi. She established her company in 2014. She leased a little takeaway restaurant close to her long-closed house. She began experimenting and trying various things at home until they were able to test the "halloumi cheese" correctly. She began to send some pieces to her English neighbours and friends in the Middle East, and she got a lot of encouragement to keep going. She faced a number of challenges. First, as an asylum seeker, she was not allowed to apply for another bank loan until she had been granted permanent residency. After that, she launched a crowdfunding campaign to raise some cash. She trusted her family and parents to look after the children. She is currently producing in a small local business with assistance from her brother and spouse.

Through the sale of produced cheese pieces, the female immigrant entrepreneur was able to achieve her financial objective. She also felt appreciated in her new country since she was asked to speak at various events held by women's organisations and universities in the UK about her experiences as an international, female, Arabic, Muslim businesswoman in Europe. She was also included on the shortlist for the 2023 Great British Entrepreneurs Awards in the Entrepreneur category. As a "purpose-driven entrepreneur," she hopes to support the general well-being of society and is thinking of "expanding the sales to several cities in the UK, maybe another European country in the future."

This case demonstrates that the motivation behind migrant and "refugee" entrepreneurship is the need to flee war, which shocks the migrant entrepreneur and her family and forces her to "eradicate" from a familiar social and cultural setting (Desai et al., 2021). She was unable to use the prior networks in her home nation to help with her "re-embeddedness" in the host nation and the opening of a new company. As a sort of eradication, Razan made the decision to launch an entirely new endeavour that would not be able to capitalise on her prior knowledge of the founder. Her love of food transcends nutrition, and her strong desire to provide for her family, which fosters resilience, serves as a compensatory mechanism. Being resilient is more than just a personal quality; it's a skill that comes with experience and adaptability to changing circumstances. It's interesting to note that, in this case, the liabilities of gender and foreignness are lessened by passion and resilience. However, the difficulties in juggling work and family obligations and raising the kids demonstrate an implicit gender liability. However, the woman's family—her parents, brother, and husband—proved to be crucial in helping her overcome these problems, demonstrating that the family, in this instance, serves as the core network that supports the entrepreneurial process and allows the woman to gradually gain recognition as a successful female entrepreneur (Evansluong et al., 2023).

REFERENCES

Al Sayah, M., Salloum, C., Lefebvre, Q., Salloum, L., & Kabbara, D. (2023). Multiculturalism and entrepreneurial expansion. *International Journal of Entrepreneurship and Small Business, 50*(2), 175–193.

Aldrich, H. E., & Cliff, J. E. (2003). The pervasive effects of family on entrepreneurship: Toward a family embeddedness perspective. *Journal of Business Venturing, 18*(5), 573–596.

Arenius, P., & Minniti, M. (2005). Perceptual variables and nascent entrepreneurship. *Small Business Economics, 24*(3), 233–247.
Barth, H., & Zalkat, G. (2020). Immigrant entrepreneurship in Sweden: The liability of newness. *Sustainability, 12*(16), 6478.
Brush, C. G., De Bruin, A., & Welter, F. (2009). A gender-aware framework for women's entrepreneurship. *International Journal of Gender and Entrepreneurship*.
Brzozowski, J., Cucculelli, M., & Surdej, A. (2017). The determinants of transnational entrepreneurship and transnational ties' dynamics among immigrant entrepreneurs in ICT sector in Italy. *International Migration, 55*(3), 105–125.
Chen, W., & Tan, J. (2009). Understanding transnational entrepreneurship through a network lens: Theoretical and methodological considerations. *Entrepreneurship Theory and Practice, 33*(5), 1079–1091.
Chreim, S., Spence, M., Crick, D., & Liao, X. L. (2018). Review of female immigrant entrepreneurship research: Past findings, gaps and ways forward. *European Management Journal, 36*(2), 210–222.
Chrysostome, E., & Lin, X. (2010). Immigrant entrepreneurship: Scrutinizing a promising type of business venture. *Thunderbird International Business Review, 52*(2), 77–82.
Cohen, R. (2008). *Global diasporas: An introduction*. Routledge.
Collins, J., & Low, A. (2010). Asian female immigrant entrepreneurs in small and medium-sized businesses in Australia. *Entrepreneurship and Regional Development, 22*(1), 97–111.
De Luca, D., & Ambrosini, M. (2019). Female immigrant entrepreneurs: More than a family strategy. *International Migration, 57*(5), 201–215.
De Vita, L., Mari, M., & Poggesi, S. (2014). Women entrepreneurs in and from developing countries: Evidences from the literature. *European Management Journal, 32*(3), 451–460.
Desai, S., Naude, W., & Stel, N. (2021). Refugee entrepreneurship: Context and directions for future research. *Small Business Economics, 56*(3), 933–945.
Discua Cruz, A., Howorth, C., & Hamilton, E. (2013). Intrafamily entrepreneurship: The formation and membership of family entrepreneurial teams. *Entrepreneurship Theory and Practice, 37*(1), 17–46.
Djelic, M.-L., & Quack, S. (2010). *Transnational communities: Shaping global economic governance*. Cambridge University Press.
Drori, I., Honig, B., & Ginsberg, A. (2006). *Transnational entrepreneurship: Toward a unifying theoretical framework*. Paper presented at the Academy of Management Proceedings.
Drori, I., Honig, B., & Wright, M. (2009). Transnational entrepreneurship: An emergent field of study. *Entrepreneurship Theory and Practice, 33*(5), 1001–1022.

Elo, M., Sandberg, S., Servais, P., Basco, R., Cruz, A. D., Riddle, L., & Täube, F. (2018). Advancing the views on migrant and diaspora entrepreneurs in international entrepreneurship. *Journal of International Entrepreneurship*, *16*(2), 119–133.

Evansluong, Q. V. D., Ramirez-Pasillas, M., Discua Cruz, A., Elo, M., & Vershinina, N. (2023). Guest editorial: Migrant entrepreneurship and the roles of family beyond place and space: Towards a family resourcefulness across borders perspective. *Journal of Enterprising Communities: People and Places in the Global Economy*, *17*(1), 1–15.

Ezzedeen, S. R., & Zikic, J. (2017). Finding balance amid boundarylessness: An interpretive study of entrepreneurial work–life balance and boundary management. *Journal of Family Issues*, *38*(11), 1546–1576.

Fong, R., Busch, N. B., Armour, M., Heffron, L. C., & Chanmugam, A. (2007). Pathways to self-sufficiency: Successful entrepreneurship for refugees. *Journal of Ethnic & Cultural Diversity in Social Work*, *16*(1-2), 127–159.

Gonzalez-Gonzalez, J. M., Bretones, F. D., Zarco, V., & Rodriguez, A. (2011). Women, immigration and entrepreneurship in Spain: A confluence of debates in the face of a complex reality. *Womens Studies International Forum*, *34*(5), 360–370.

Gurău, C., Dana, L. P., & Light, I. (2020). Overcoming the liability of foreignness: A typology and model of immigrant entrepreneurs. *European Management Review*, *17*(3), 701–717.

Gusfield, J. R. (1975). *Community: A critical response*. Harper & Row New York.

Hong, Y.-y., Morris, M. W., Chiu, C.-Y., & Benet-Martinez, V. (2000). Multicultural minds: A dynamic constructivist approach to culture and cognition. *American Psychologist*, *55*(7), 709.

Kabbara, D. (2009). The evolutionary network process of international entrepreneurial firms. *International Journal of Globalisation and Small Business*, *3*(3), 346–370.

Kabbara, D. (2023). Female entrepreneurship: Typologies, drivers and value creation. In *New horizons and global perspectives in female entrepreneurship research* (pp. 93–112). Emerald Publishing Limited.

Kabbara, D., & Zucchella, A. (2023). Transnational entrepreneurship. Insights from female entrepreneurs in the modest fashion industry. *Journal of International Management*, *29*(5), 101058.

Kabbara, D., Suárez-Ortega, S. M., & Zucchella, A. (2025). Developing entrepreneurial opportunities through multi-layered liabilities: the experiences of female migrant entrepreneurs. *The International Entrepreneurship and Management Journal*, *21*(1), 1–32. https://doi.org/10.1007/s11365-024-01010-3.

Kalleberg, A. L., & Leicht, K. T. (1991). Gender and organizational performance: Determinants of small business survival and success. *Academy of Management Journal*, *34*(1), 136–161.

Kerr, S. P., & Kerr, W. (2020). Immigrant entrepreneurship in America: Evidence from the survey of business owners 2007 & 2012. *Research Policy, 49*(3), 103918.

Kloosterman, R., Van der Leun, J., & Rath, J. (1998). Across the border: Immigrants' economic opportunities, social capital and informal business activities. *Journal of Ethnic and Migration Studies, 24*(2), 249–268.

Kogan, I. (2006). Labor markets and economic incorporation among recent immigrants in Europe. *Social Forces, 85*(2), 697–721.

Kumar, P., Deodhar, S. J., & Zaheer, S. (2022). Cognitive sources of liability of foreignness in crowdsourcing creative work. *Journal of International Business Studies*, 1–31.

Levitt, P., & Schiller, N. G. (2004). Conceptualizing simultaneity: A transnational social field perspective on society 1. *International Migration Review, 38*(3), 1002–1039.

Lindley, A. (2009). The early-morning phonecall: Remittances from a refugee diaspora perspective. *Journal of Ethnic and Migration Studies, 35*(8), 1315–1334.

Lissoni, F. (2018). International migration and innovation diffusion: An eclectic survey. *Regional Studies, 52*(5), 702–714.

Marchand, K., Siegel, M., Kuschminder, K., Majidi, N., Vanore, M., & Buil, C. (2014). *Afghanistan migration profile*. International Organization for Migration.

McAdam, M., Harrison, R. T., & Leitch, C. M. (2019). Stories from the field: Women's networking as gender capital in entrepreneurial ecosystems. *Small Business Economics, 53*(2), 459–474.

McDougall, P. P., & Oviatt, B. M. (2000). International entrepreneurship: The intersection of two research paths. *Academy of Management Journal, 43*(5), 902–906.

Morgan, H. M., Sui, S., & Malhotra, S. (2021). No place like home: The effect of exporting to the country of origin on the financial performance of immigrant-owned SMEs. *Journal of International Business Studies, 52*(3), 504–524.

Moufakkir, O. (2020). Experience of Arab/Muslim women visiting relatives in the West and the management of stigma by association. *Tourism Management, 78*, 104073.

Munkejord, M. C. (2017). Local and transnational networking among female immigrant entrepreneurs in peripheral rural contexts: perspectives on Russians in Finnmark, Norway. *Eur. Urban Reg. Stud. 24*(1), 7–20. https://doi.org/10.1177/0969776415587122.

Mustafa, M., & Chen, S. (2010). The strength of family networks in transnational immigrant entrepreneurship. *Thunderbird Int. Bus. Rev. 52*(2), 97–106. https://doi.org/10.1002/tie.20317.

Oviatt, B. M., & McDougall, P. P. (1997). Challenges for internationalization process theory: The case of international new ventures. *MIR: Management International Review, 37*, 85–99.

Oviatt, B. M., & McDougall, P. P. (2005). Defining international entrepreneurship and modeling the speed of internationalization. *Entrepreneurship Theory and Practice, 29*(5), 537–553.

Parrilli, M. D., Montresor, S., & Trippl, M. (2019). A new approach to migrations: Communities-on-the-move as assets. *Regional Studies, 53*(1), 1–5.

Phizacklea, A., & Ram, M. (1996). Being your own boss: Ethnic minority entrepreneurs in comparative perspective. *Work, Employment and Society, 10*(2), 319–339.

Poggesi, S., Mari, M., & De Vita, L. (2016). What's new in female entrepreneurship research? Answers from the literature. *International Entrepreneurship and Management Journal, 12*(3), 735–764.

Pruthi, S., Basu, A., & Wright, M. (2018). Ethnic ties, motivations, and home country entry strategy of transnational entrepreneurs. *J. Int. Entrep. 16*(2), 210–243. https://doi.org/10.1007/s10843-017-0223-2.

Rath, J., & Kloosterman, R. (2000). Outsiders' business: A critical review of research on immigrant entrepreneurship. *International Migration Review, 34*(3), 657–681.

Rindova, V., Barry, D., & Ketchen, D. J., Jr. (2009). Entrepreneuring as emancipation. *Academy of Management Review, 34*(3), 477–491.

Rovai, A. P. (2002). Building sense of community at a distance. *The International Review of Research in Open and Distributed Learning, 3*(1).

Safran, W. (1991). Diasporas in modern societies: Myths of homeland and return. *Diaspora: A Journal of Transnational Studies, 1*(1), 83–99.

Saxton, T., Wesley, C. L., & Saxton, M. K. (2016). Venture advocate behaviors and the emerging enterprise. *Strategic Entrepreneurship Journal, 10*(1), 107–125.

Shepherd, D. (2015). Party On! A call for entrepreneurship research that is more interactive, activity based, cognitively hot, compassionate, and prosocial. *Journal of Business Venturing, 30*(4), 489–507.

Shepherd, D. A., Saade, F. P., & Wincent, J. (2019). How to circumvent adversity? Refugee-entrepreneurs' resilience in the face of substantial and persistent adversity. *Journal of Business Venturing, 35*, 105940.

Solano, G. (2020). The mixed embeddedness of transnational migrant entrepreneurs: Moroccans in Amsterdam and Milan. *Journal of Ethnic and Migration Studies, 46*(10), 2067–2085.

Stinchcombe, A. L. (1965). Organizations and social structure. *Handbook of Organizations, 44*(2), 142–193.

Suárez-Ortega, S. M., & García-Cabrera, A. M. (2022). The Western immigrant as tourism entrepreneur in Morocco. *Annals of Tourism Research Empirical Insights, 3*(2), 100058.

Waldinger, R. D., Aldrich, H., & Ward, R. (1990). *Ethnic entrepreneurs: Immigrant business in industrial societies* (Vol. Vol. 1). Sage Publications, Inc.

Wauters, B., & Lambrecht, J. (2008). Barriers to refugee entrepreneurship in Belgium: Towards an explanatory model. *Journal of Ethnic and Migration Studies, 34*(6), 895–915.

Yinger, J. M. (1994). *Ethnicity: Source of strength? Source of conflict?* Suny Press.

Zahra, S. A., & George, G. (2002). International entrepreneurship: The current status of the field and future research agenda. In *Strategic entrepreneurship: Creating a new mindset* (pp. 255–288). Blackwell Publishers.

Zahra, S. A., Wright, M., & Abdelgawad, S. G. (2014). Contextualization and the advancement of entrepreneurship research. *International Small Business Journal, 32*(5), 479–500.

Zhou, M. (2004). Revisiting ethnic entrepreneurship: Convergencies, controversies, and conceptual Advancements 1. *International Migration Review, 38*(3), 1040–1074.

Zolin, R., & Schlosser, F. (2013). Characteristics of immigrant entrepreneurs and their involvement in international new ventures. *Thunderbird International Business Review, 55*(3), 271–284.

Zucchella, A., & Kabbara, D. (2011). Collaborative entrepreneurship and internationalization in life sciences: Global growth through collaboration in Italian biotech firms. In *International entrepreneurship in the life sciences*. Edward Elgar Publishing.

Zucchella, A., & Kabbara, D. (2013). The role of partnerships in the internationalisation process of small knowledge intensive firms (SKIFs). *Management International/International Management/Gestión Internacional, 18*(1), 104–116.

Conclusion

The global transformation has affected every business across all industries and is independent of the manager's or entrepreneur's gender. This book illustrates how global disruptions and transformations have created challenges and opportunities for transformative entrepreneurs, not only male entrepreneurs but also female entrepreneurs around the globe. Global transformation and transformative entrepreneurship around the globe have also affected female entrepreneurial activities and empowered female entrepreneurship. The phenomenon of global transformation and transformative entrepreneurship has had a notable impact on female entrepreneurship and empowered female entrepreneurs globally. This book, through its six chapters, illustrates how it entails adapting female entrepreneurs to global transformation; these strategies include (1) empowering female entrepreneurship, (2) engaging in the informal economy, (3) embracing new digital technologies, (4) integrating sustainable practices and business models, and (5) Engaging in migrant entrepreneurship. The author overviewed different practices of transformation in a number of female cases in different countries, including their strengths and weaknesses, the opportunities they addressed, and the threats they have to face. The book also revealed the transformative and emancipatory nature of the entrepreneurial experience for female entrepreneurs in light of the recent global transformation.

Female entrepreneurship has a major impact on economic development and is recognised as a key factor in innovation and job creation. The pursuit of female entrepreneurship involves more than just generating wealth and jobs. The female entrepreneur is viewed as a functional individual managing a business as well as a representative of humanity (pursuing personal goals). The female entrepreneur is viewed as a functional individual in charge of the economic, social, and financial performance of a company, as well as a representative of humanity (pursuing personal goals). Social entrepreneurship's result is the creation of societal value. It is regarded as a behavioural phenomenon that transcends the economic sphere, and the social dimension of the phenomenon predominates over non-economic values. Compared to men, female entrepreneurs are more likely to prioritise social value creation over economic value creation and to follow social values in their business endeavours.

Entrepreneurship has been acknowledged as a potential solution to major social and environmental issues like climate change. The emerging field of sustainable and circular entrepreneurship is a powerful factor in the creation of innovative and desirable value for humankind and the earth. This book recognises how female entrepreneurs pay particular attention to sustainability and address environmental entrepreneurial goals as they have entrepreneurial intentions in sustainable entrepreneurship. They have demonstrated their entrepreneurial intentions by following a waste minimisation practice and enhancing the quality of life.

This book also shows how being a member of an ethnic minority in the host nation can present additional difficulties for female immigrant entrepreneurs, such as "cultural" discrimination from the majority population. In this situation, they must rely on both their family networks and the ethnic community network. People who bring their cultural heritage and similar values and beliefs that encourage cooperation and trust make up a community of shared values in the host nation. These ethnic groups might be able to assist female immigrant business owners in pursuing their ventures. Using the networks of their families and communities, female immigrant entrepreneurs helped to create social value in the host country through their businesses. For example, they could devise strategies to address social issues in the receiving nations. Thus, the community and the environment at large were impacted by this creation of social and environmental values. Female immigrant entrepreneurs could find opportunities for community service, female leadership, and social advancement in their host countries by participating in the creation of social value. The economic value generated was essential to fulfilling the two main goals of female immigrant entrepreneurs: the creation of jobs that recognised and empowered them and compensated their families for their support, as well as economic autonomy.

When starting their businesses, female digital entrepreneurs must rely on social networks (apart from the family social network). They typically rely on social media as a vital networking tool to build social capital, broaden their participation internationally, and interact with clients. When launching a business, social media's self-generating and responsive platforms can assist female entrepreneurs in overcoming obstacles to market access. Social media platforms are crucial in helping women start their own home-based businesses. Through their businesses, female digital entrepreneurs have made a positive impact on society and the world economy by leveraging their social media networks. Social interaction in social media empowers female entrepreneurs personally and in relationships with others, as well as within the larger community. Specifically, it improves their capacity for expression, increases the amount of experience that women share, and increases the degree to which they feel empowered to face and transform their challenging circumstances. Additionally, by joining a larger social network, Social media minimises their isolation, boosts their social capital, and enhances their community involvement (Cesaroni et al., 2017). In terms of the economy, female digital entrepreneurs increase household income, which strengthens their ability to negotiate and bargain for changes made in the home and, by reducing unemployment, allows more socially marginalised individuals to participate in the economy. However, female entrepreneurs also need to consider the negative aspects of technology, such as unfavourable remarks on social media.

Furthermore, the book disclosed that female sustainable entrepreneurs may encounter financial difficulties due to competition from rivals who prioritise cutting costs associated with raw materials and optimising profits through large-scale production. For these business owners, "The first step towards ending past partnerships could be developing a circular business model. In certain instances, this shift necessitates that businesses enhance their material selection and replace their present input source with pure, nontoxic raw materials. For example, in order to comply with the United Nations Sustainable Goals agenda, they exhibit professional and ethical traits and choose to adopt circular business models and sustainable practices within their organisations. Additionally, this book disclosed that female sustainable business owners could encounter financial challenges;

consequently, because they were motivated by prosocial motivation to make a positive impact on the world and the planet, female resilient entrepreneurs also contribute to the creation of environmental value. These business owners might have trouble finding investors who understand the market potential of their venture and who have similar sustainable goals. In such instances, technology and crowdfunding platforms were crucial sources of initial funding for female sustainable entrepreneurs, and they also served as a means of evaluating the business idea's value proposition. Their sustainable model might attract investors and citizens who are willing to make small financial commitments to support a circular economy concept. To close the loop in the circular economy, engaging in entrepreneurial activities related to circular entrepreneurship necessitates partnerships and collaborations with multiple stakeholders. Since they are regarded as vital and engaged members of the sustainable entrepreneurial ecosystem, these business relationships also extend to suppliers and organisations further up the value chain as well as end users. Prosocial and intrinsic motivations combine to drive female sustainable entrepreneurs to pursue their businesses. Although they were driven by a desire to help the environment and the planet, they were also motivated by a desire for self-fulfilment. The generation of social and economic value is inextricably linked to the creation of environmental value. The use of sustainable practices in product development and manufacturing has become increasingly important to female sustainable entrepreneurs. In an effort to minimise their impact on the environment, female entrepreneurs focused on utilising natural materials in their products and adhering to a waste management strategy. Suppliers and organisations throughout the value chain are included in these business relationships, and even female sustainable entrepreneurs have addressed social and environmental goals more than economic ones. Since they embrace multiple objectives (people and planet), they view long-term profit as a necessary but not sufficient condition for their existence.

This book has revealed that balancing work and family responsibilities is one of the most significant challenges female entrepreneurs face in their entrepreneurial endeavours. This leads to their subsequent hunt for a job that is suitable and flexible in order to maintain a work-life balance. Because of this, female entrepreneurs adopted new business strategies in the digital age by utilising digital transformation, technology breakthroughs, and the evolution of digitalisation. Internet business creation requires little capital and operating expenses for female entrepreneurs in low-income nations. Many organisations' strategic goals and managers have shifted from a so-called "quest for profits" to a "quest for resilience" as a result of the increased disruptions in the global economy, market volatility, and environmental disasters. Utilising their inventiveness, female entrepreneurs innovate out of need and provide game-changing answers to the issues they encounter. As a result, they helped to create value in the social, economic, and environmental spheres. Because of their high resilience and self-efficacy, they were able to succeed as entrepreneurs as their male counterparts and to find opportunities for female leadership at the social level. In order for them to achieve financial independence and survival during the disruptive period, the economic value they produced was crucial, and it also served as compensation for their families' support during these trying times.

Given the rise of global transformation and the female entrepreneurs operating in the global economy, the book is timely and highly pertinent and has several implications for policy intervention as policymakers in various regions are becoming more aware of the global transformation trend. This calls for a dialogue between firms, female entrepreneurs and institutions, all of which must coevolve in the direction of adapting to global transformation.

First, institutional context from a perceptual and gendered perspective explains how policymakers need to combine rules and policies with adequate communication, specifically targeting female understanding of institutional barriers. Hence, there is a need for government services to communicate through female entrepreneurship agencies and raise female entrepreneurs's awareness of laws and regulations linked to entrepreneurship. Second, the book stresses the relationship between digital transformation and the technological context with female entrepreneurs. It recognises that female entrepreneurs leverage digital technologies for education, learning, and acquiring new (digital) skills. Entrepreneurial education and training are needed. Hence, policymakers can provide (online) training courses and mentoring programs to help female entrepreneurs develop soft entrepreneurial skills, such as addressing a lack of self-confidence. Third, female entrepreneurs may encounter tensions and stress caused by dealing with negative online comments while leveraging the technological context to explore and exploit entrepreneurial opportunities. Creating a call centre or specific programs to provide some psychological support and empower the emotional intelligence of female entrepreneurs would help them overcome these tensions caused by the technological context. This support would help build social connections and professional inclusion of female entrepreneurs. More specifically, they should promote mentorship programs with successful cases of female entrepreneurs globally who are working in several industries. Fourth, Improving the female entrepreneur's proficiency with digital tools is essential to providing specialised professional courses on how to become proficient in mobile product photography and boosting sales on social media, mainly for females working in the digital field.

In addition, since the book shows that female entrepreneurs face obstacles in obtaining capital and drawing investors, local funding programs for female entrepreneurs should be established in order to support their business endeavours. The book also demonstrates that most female entrepreneurs (primarily in developing nations) had no prior business experience when they launched their companies. Training courses and mentorship programs are required to assist female entrepreneurs—mostly immigrants—in developing their entrepreneurial skills. Therefore, policymakers can help female immigrants develop their entrepreneurial skills by offering them education and mentoring. These programs will facilitate the building of social networks, self-assurance, and inclusion in the workforce and economy. In addition, they would guarantee links to mainstream infrastructures and promote networks of entrepreneurs. An international female entrepreneur must recognise and comprehend the laws and regulations of the new nation before opening for business. Government services, like workshops, are therefore required in order to increase the awareness of host country regulations among female international (migrant) entrepreneurs. These services might offer information (in a variety of languages) on important administrative laws and rules, as well as the prerequisites for setting up and running a company in a foreign nation. Policymakers should assist and encourage female entrepreneurs who prioritise sustainability in their businesses by offering incentives during the procurement process, as the book shows how female-owned businesses would benefit from implementing sustainability. These benefits are represented by increasing the number of employees, creating jobs for women in the nation, and gaining a reputation for sustainability on a global scale. These services might offer some financial resources to start a long-lasting business. Additionally, by providing sustainable products with a competitive edge, policymakers can recommend environmental taxes to assist sustainable entrepreneurs in gaining market share. Government policy must address the various obstacles that female entrepreneurs face in their pursuit of entrepreneurship, including those relating to skills and credit availability, the digital age (such as illiteracy and lack of technological aptitude), context-specific issues (such as gender equality and the absence of legislation), and providing support for these obstacles. For example, government policy should support women entrepreneurs by offering training, mentorship, financial matching, and business matching. It should also build digital capacity, increase women entrepreneurs' knowledge of digital technology, and enact laws that will empower women entrepreneurs in the digital space. More precisely, in the digital age, government policy affects women's entrepreneurial ecosystems. The book also explains that the degree of female digital skills, access to digital finance, involvement in accelerator and incubation programs, and government support for promoting national digital entrepreneurship are all indicators of the involvement of women entrepreneurs in the emerging digital economy. Because of technological advancements, the network of female entrepreneurs became more globally and locally connected, resulting in a geographically dispersed social circle. Online communication enables people to cross national boundaries and create long-distance social networks without physically moving across borders through blogs and digital media (Jafari-Sadeghi et al., 2021).

Regarding managerial implications, the book can encourage female entrepreneurs and managers to consider the circumstances surrounding the creation of international opportunities in light of the upheavals and changes occurring throughout the world. It is imperative for female entrepreneurs to enhance and broaden their networks with stakeholders, whether through digital platforms or local cultural events. This book recognises the value of digital platforms for cross-border opportunity exploration and exploitation. Female entrepreneurs must rely on social media to grow their businesses into new international markets, raise their brand awareness worldwide, and enhance their global sales. Furthermore, by implementing a circular business model within their companies, female entrepreneurs can establish born circular firms.

References

Cesaroni, F. M., Demartini, P., & Paoloni, P. (2017). Women in business and social media: Implications for female entrepreneurship in emerging countries. *African Journal of Business Management, 11*(14), 316–326.

Jafari-Sadeghi, V., Garcia-Perez, A., Candelo, E., & Couturier, J. (2021). Exploring the impact of digital transformation on technology entrepreneurship and technological market expansion: The role of technology readiness, exploration and exploitation. *Journal of Business research, 124*, 100–111.

Index

A
Artificial intelligence (AI), ix, 5, 18–21, 23, 52, 66

B
Born circular firm, 92–93, 97, 141
Born-global firms, 47, 49

C
Chiara Ferragni, 76–80
Circular business model, 88, 90–92, 102, 105, 137, 141
Circular economy, 5, 24, 86–93, 97–102, 105–107, 138
Circular entrepreneurship, 89–90, 101, 102, 136, 138
Climate change, 2, 4, 5, 11, 15, 17–18, 24, 28, 71, 87, 96, 98, 100, 101, 104, 114, 136
COÉGA, 102–105
Community, 10, 13, 23, 24, 26, 28, 37, 39, 41, 53, 54, 74, 86, 87, 91, 93, 96, 104, 114, 119–123, 125, 127, 136, 137
COVID-19, 2, 16–17, 52, 73
Culture, 5, 18, 22, 26, 28, 38, 44, 45, 78, 98, 99, 101, 114, 116, 119, 122–125, 127
Cyberbullying, 75
Cyberfeminism, 69, 70, 73

D
Digitalisation, viii, 14, 18, 19, 50, 51, 68, 138
Digital platforms, 5, 19, 55, 64–66, 69–74, 76, 80, 141
Digital transformation (DT), vii, viii, 5, 19–23, 52, 64–66, 71, 75, 76, 138, 139

E
Economic autonomy, 125, 137
Ecopreneurship, 95–97, 99
Emancipation, 2, 41, 119

Environmental sustainability, 2, 50, 95, 96
Eradication, 129
Ethnic minorities, 13, 123, 136

F
Family network, 37, 120–121, 136
Fashion industry, 76, 100–103

G
Gender, viii, 2–4, 28, 38, 42, 56, 67, 68, 70, 73, 94, 96, 97, 123, 124, 129, 135
Gender equality, 2, 4, 36, 96
Global disruptions, 2, 3, 15–21, 135

H
Huda Kattan Beauty, 52–56

I
Inclusion, vii, viii, 23, 26, 27, 66–70, 73, 75, 119, 140
Inclusive entrepreneurship, 13–14, 66–68
Influencer, 73–80, 105
Informal economy, 2, 14, 15, 67, 76, 135
Informal entrepreneurship, 14–15, 69, 76
Innovation, vii–ix, 2, 11, 12, 21, 22, 26, 36, 39, 45, 46, 50, 53–56, 64, 65, 67, 68, 89, 90, 93, 98, 100, 101, 103, 114, 116, 119, 125, 136
Instagram, 53, 69, 71, 77
International entrepreneurship, viii, 5, 11, 12, 24, 36, 38, 43–48, 50, 66, 114–117, 120
Internationalisation, 2, 5, 11, 18, 36, 37, 41, 43, 44, 46, 47, 49, 56, 80, 119, 120

Intrinsic motivation, 101, 105, 127, 138

L
Liabilities, 5, 22, 28, 29, 43, 49, 56, 64, 79, 80, 124, 129

M
Marginalised people, 3
Migrant entrepreneurship, viii, 27, 28, 116, 119–123, 127, 135
Migration, 2, 4, 5, 14, 26–29, 40, 41, 43, 114–117, 120, 124, 128

O
Opportunities, vii–ix, 2, 3, 5, 10, 11, 13–15, 17, 22, 29, 36, 39, 41, 42, 47, 49–51, 64–66, 68–71, 74, 87, 89, 92–94, 96, 98, 105, 114–116, 119, 121–127, 135, 136, 139, 141

P
Prosocial motivation, 97, 138

S
Social media, 5, 52, 54, 55, 66–71, 73–76, 79, 105, 137, 140, 141
Social recognition, 125
Social transformation, 21, 26–29
Sustainability, vii, viii, 2, 14, 15, 17, 18, 22–26, 50, 66, 86, 87, 89, 90, 92–99, 101–103, 136, 140
Sustainable Development Goals (SDGs), 2, 4, 5, 16, 96
Sustainable entrepreneurship, 24, 86–107, 136

Sustainable transformation, 4–5, 21, 23–26

T
Transformative entrepreneurship, vii–ix, 3–5, 10–29, 36, 86–93, 114–129, 135

U
Unicorns start-ups, 48–52

V
Vulnerability, 123

W
Work life balance, 15, 72, 138

Y
Yorkshire Damacheese, 125–127

GPSR Compliance

The European Union's (EU) General Product Safety Regulation (GPSR) is a set of rules that requires consumer products to be safe and our obligations to ensure this.

If you have any concerns about our products, you can contact us on ProductSafety@springernature.com

In case Publisher is established outside the EU, the EU authorized representative is:

Springer Nature Customer Service Center GmbH
Europaplatz 3
69115 Heidelberg, Germany

Batch number: 08158396

Printed by Printforce, the Netherlands